The Song of Songs
and
Enlightenment

Also by Dorothy Elder

REVELATION: FOR A NEW AGE
(The Book of Revelation)

WOMEN OF THE BIBLE SPEAK TO
WOMEN OF TODAY

The Song of Songs and Enlightenment

A Metaphysical Interpretation

DOROTHY ELDER

DeVorss & Company
P.O. Box 550, Marina del Rey, CA 90294-0550

ISBN: 0-87516-611-3
Library of Congress Catalog Card Number: 88-72028

Printed in the United States of America

Contents

Dedicated to
All Seekers on the Path
to
Enlightenment

Preface

The Song of Songs is a short book of only eight chapters. It is said to have been written by Solomon, the famous king of Judah, whose father, David, was a great patriarch. However, for the purposes of this book it is not important who recorded it or when it was written. The Song of Songs is for mankind of all ages, climes, and religions, and it is as true and timely now as when it was written.

We all vibrate to song. This Song is "pure" music, and we each provide the melody, harmony, and rhythm as we read it from the metaphysical viewpoint, unlocking its secrets by seeing it as symbolic. We are then swept up to a higher awareness of our own Divinity and the ultimate state of our Oneness with God. Thus the Song of Songs has a personal and Universal meaning.

This interpretation of the Song can be classified as mystical. Throughout, I see the individual Soul seeking union with the God or Universal Love that mankind has paid such homage to. This is the secret of our seeking, for we are all seeking. We are seeking a final state of Oneness with God, and are fast approaching the time when more and more of us will experience the ecstasy of completion.

My own very simple definition of a mystic is one who is centered on the Hidden Splendor within, who listens to and follows the guidance of this Inner Knowing and whose life is committed to Oneness with God or whatever word is used to describe that One Energy that flows through and surrounds us all.

The end point of mysticism is thus an exalted awareness of God at all times, which brings ecstasy and joy beyond most human understanding.

My thesis is that the Song of Songs describes the coming together of the masculine and feminine within the consciousness of the individual. When this occurs, there is no duality, no attachment to anyone on earth. No obstacle lies between the individual Soul and Oneness with God, and that Oneness will be such ecstasy that it cannot be compared to physical sexual ecstasy, for it has no division. It is One. The Song therefore has both practical and mystical applications. It not only guides us to that high state of consciousness, but it tells us how to get there.

Hundreds of books have been written on this Song of Songs, many of them interpreting it as a description of physical love between a maid and a boy. Others see it as describing the relationship between the Israelites and Jehovah, or the relationship between the Church and Jesus Christ.

The basis of this interpretation, however, is the acceptance that it is the story of a Bride and a Bridegroom dancing the celestial dance that ultimately reaches a climax in the Mystical Marriage, or Enlightenment. The Bride, in my interpretation, is the Soul of each of us, and the Bridegroom is that Universal Energy that calls us to wholeness.

To better understand what I am going to offer, I should like to suggest that the Song is given in four divisions. These are not clear-cut—one spills over into the other—but they give us some form or organization. They are really

the four steps of Love, for this is a Love poem, and it
teaches us about that great mystery. The steps* are:

1. Betrothal, or Conversion
2. Marriage; pure contemplation
3. Union; confirmation in mystic life; Mystic Marriage;
   Enlightenment
4. Fruitfulness of the Soul; co-creation with God; Service

Each of these stages needs some explanation.

A real *Conversion* is a unique experience which includes
the Soul, body, mind, and emotions. It lifts one above the
world and turns one's whole life around, so that one finds
new direction for going on. This is the beginning of a high
awareness, within the person, of his own Divinity and that
of mankind. He is beginning the process of Enlightenment.

My own conversion in this lifetime came when I was a
wife and mother of three children. I was deeply unhappy
in my marriage and I had not expressed my real self,
although I did not know who that was. I prayed, on my
knees, to a God I was not sure of.

A Being of Light answered. I had never had a vision and
didn't really believe anyone ever did. But this Being of
Light came and touched me and gave me the thought, "I
will be with you in all your problems." I was over-
whelmed, for it was the most Real experience I had ever
had. And then I *knew* God at that moment. I was Converted. For the rest of the day, and for some time after, I
was in ecstasy. I kept it a secret, for there was no one to
share it with.

The Conversion was Real, and I prayed to God with deep
conviction after that. It was only years later, and after

*Richard of St. Victor's "steep stairway of love," described in Evelyn
Underhill, *Mysticism* (New York: New American Library, 1911/1955),
pp. 139, 140.

many problems, that I became knowledgeable about Contemplation and had an understanding of the experience. But I was Converted, I was changed. I was starting my conscious Spiritual Journey in this lifetime.

Your own Conversion may come from any direction or experience, but it will be absolutely personal, for your Soul is that unique Spark finding its way back to the Godhead, and it must follow its own guidance.

The next stage, *Marriage*, is reached through Contemplation. This is the beginning stage of Marriage; consummation comes later. At this stage the aspirant is confirmed in the the mystic way and has fully taken on the desire to express in pure love. Irreversible vows of marriage are made between the Soul and God. More and more illuminative experiences occur.

The third stage is called *Union* or Wedlock or the Unitive Way or Enlightenment. This is the consummation of the vows—the Mystic Marriage—the stage of becoming One with God. Life changes tremendously. One becomes a mystic.

The Journey is not finished, however. The fourth stage is *Fruitfulness*, creativity, co-creation, service. It may bring pain, suffering, duties, but this suffering will not be useless or nonproductive. It will be for the uplift of mankind, of womankind.

I see these four stages in the life of Jesus. He, our Teacher and Wayshower, is with each of us as we find our way. My wish is that this great Song will give you an insight into your own personal Way.

NOTE: Because the Song of Songs is an ancient Hebrew text, it follows the convention of regarding God as masculine. I have followed this convention in references to God, although in places I refer to God as He/She.

The Song of Songs
and
Enlightenment

Chapter One of
The Song of Songs

Chapter 1, verse 1, reads:

The Song of Songs, which is Solomon's.

Solomon symbolizes the Universal God. Each of us has this spark of the Divine within. Indeed, we *are* the Divine. We are mistaken when we think we are the body or the mind. For primarily we are Spirit.

Sol is light; *o* is glory; *mon* is Truth. *Solomon* symbolizes love and wisdom, whole and complete. The man Solomon did not always express in this way or live up to his name. Many of us have names that we don't always live up to. For the purpose of this interpretation, we will see the name of Solomon as meaning Universal God.

This is His Song of Songs. It is His teaching to us of how to achieve this high state of Oneness with Love and Wisdom or whatever your definition of God may be. It is His Song. Solomon is ever waiting for our return to Oneness and in this Song of Songs we shall be given a description of the process.

NOTE: Except where indicated, the Bible text is that of the Revised Standard Version.

1

Verses 2–7 are spoken by the maiden, the Beloved, the Soul.

VERSE 2

O that you would kiss me with the kisses of your
     mouth!
For your love is better than wine,

The maiden's love for the Lover starts with physical expressions. The kisses of our God are "sweeter than wine." Wine symbolizes the connecting link between soul and body. The blending of the two, the Soul and God, is a Wedding. Nothing physical can compare.

VERSE 3

your anointing oils are fragrant,
your name is oil poured out;
     therefore the maidens love you.

Anointing with oil refers to the spirit of love from God that is poured out upon the aspirant to make the searcher holy. The *name* referred to is what we name that Spirit that is over and in all. It is Light and Love. It is the Creator that is longing for a Marriage with each Soul. There is much holiness in the names *God* and *Jesus Christ*.

VERSE 4

Draw me after you, let us make haste.
     The King has brought me into his chambers.
We will exult and rejoice in you.

The King at the time this was written was considered to be God's representative on earth. So God has brought the speaker into his consciousness (chambers), for that is how our consciousness of love happens. That is our betrothal.

We open to the grace of God. We allow God to "draw me after You." And our love, our feeling of love, makes us exult and rejoice.

The Bride continues to speak:

VERSE 5

> I am very dark, but comely,
>> like the tents of Kedar,
>> like the curtains of Solomon.

This verse introduces that part of us that has kept our consciousness from fully realizing the Spirit within, God, from bringing us to the chamber of love. It is our shadow ("I am very dark").

Carl Jung calls the dark maiden the shadow over the Soul, that which must be removed before we are fully conscious of our Divinity. According to Jung's teaching, each of us has a shadow and maybe more than one. This is some feeling or belief that prevents us from expressing on the level of perfection we all long for. The shadow is often blamed on others. We project that which we know unconsciously about ourselves, but do not like, onto others. In this case the sun and the brothers are blamed (see Verse 6).

Our consciousness of our divinity, which lies within our Soul, is made dim by the shadows that overlie it. Cleansing of these shadows is necessary for our Enlightenment to occur.

VERSE 6

> Do not gaze at me because I am swarthy,
>> because the sun has scorched me.
> My mother's sons were angry with me,
>> they made me keeper of the vineyards;
>> but, my own vineyard I have not kept!

The sun is a symbol for Universal Energy and Light. The Egyptians taught (at least some did) that the sun is the totality of Spirit and that when the human is purified, the Soul will return to the sun. The Hebrews held God, the sun, responsible for the good and the bad that happened to them. The speaker seems to be doing the same. We tend to blame God, our parents, society, religion, race-consciousness for our shadow, which keeps our good from us. This must be overcome if we are to have the Marriage.

The Soul, the feminine, is being betrothed to the Christ, the masculine. Or in Eastern religious terms, the Divine Energy, Kundalini (Shiva), is seeking Oneness with Universal Love or God (Shakti). All separation must be overcome.

Also "mother's sons" has an esoteric meaning. Again we look for someone or something to explain our shadow. The sons being masculine are referring to the animus within the woman's consciousness, which is often negative. An animus is the masculine quality in the woman. (In the man the opposite quality is the anima.) When a woman's psyche is caught in a negative view of the masculine, she is deprived of the goal of the Mystical Marriage. This also applies to men and the feminine within them. Carl Jung speaks of this a great deal in his writings. The Soul, however, is always considered feminine, both in men and in women.

And so the Soul, the feminine, needs to see the masculine in a positive light, for God is androgynous, and to be at One we must accept our feminine and our masculine as being positive aspects of our psyche. We cannot blame the males or the females in our life for our shadow. We need to rid ourselves of it.

The vine, according to Corinne Heline, represents aspiration or idealism. We all have the vine, for we all have aspirations for a higher level of being. But our shadow can become very large when we are keeping the vineyards of others. We realize we have not kept our own vineyard and thus have become darker. This is almost an expression of repentance, a confession.

VERSE 7

Tell me, you whom my soul loves,
    where you pasture your flock,
    where you make it lie down at noon;
for why should I be like one who wanders
    beside the flocks of your companions?

"Tell me, you whom my soul loves" is a direct request to the Christ of love that our deepest spiritual being, the Soul, wants to find.

Jesus called himself the good shepherd. Shepherd means wise teacher. Jesus and God were One. God is our shepherd. "The Lord is my Shepherd" is the first line of the oft-spoken Twenty-third Psalm. So the feminine is appealing to God to show where she can find Him.

The search for God goes on and on in our lives until we find Him. There is a built-in discontent that pushes us into many experiences on earth which seem to fill the need. Sex, work, activity, sports, money, lovers, friends, wife or husband, children, beauty of possessions, books, jewels, etc., etc. But none of this satisfies. It is God we are searching for.

The speaker is saying, "Give me a more direct route to your Presence. Why should I wander around? I want you and do not need to wander in search of you."

"Flocks" also refer to thoughts. Our thoughts are often our greatest nemesis when searching for God. Our thoughts are companions with God but may not be focused on our spiritual development. The flocks, the thoughts of God, are pastured right within our own thinking process. It is giving up our usual thoughts and focusing upon God that brings our conversion.

Remember in my personal account of conversion (see the preface), I spoke to what I thought might exist but wasn't sure did, and said in effect, "I give up. Come to me." That brings conversion.

The Lover speaks:

VERSES 8–11

If you do not know,
   O fairest among women,
follow in the tracks of the flock,
   and pasture your kids
   beside the shepherds' tents.
I compare you, my love,
   to a mare of Pharaoh's chariots.
Your cheeks are comely with ornaments,
   your neck with strings of jewels,
We will make you ornaments of gold,
   studded with silver.

In these verses is the reply from the masculine principle, which is within each of us. This principle is aggressive, is the will, is the power of desiring. We need to heed this principle.

In Verse 8 he is following up her inquiry of Verse 7, which asks where he can be found. The answer is "follow the tracks of the flocks [thoughts]" and "pasture your kids [young searching thoughts] beside the shepherds' tents."

The tents are not permanent structures. "Tent" refers to consciousness, and so she is being told that her early thoughts of Oneness with the masculine principle will be tentative, weak, childish, young. The shepherd, wise teacher, dwells in temporary states of mind at this point.

Verse 9: The most beautiful, rhythmic, sleek, highly intelligent, expertly trained mare would be pulling the Pharaoh's chariot. She would be a picture of beauty. God woos us, if we will listen, by telling us that our Soul is of the highest quality. Often we ignore the perfection that lies hidden within our consciousness. It should be guiding our perfect body (Pharaoh's chariot). Our body carries our Soul; some maintain that the body is *in* the Soul.

In Verses 10 and 11 the Soul is here described as beautiful with jewels (spiritual truths) and will be more beautiful when silver (reflection of the divine feminine) and gold (divine masculine intelligence) are recognized. All of these Truths that come to us through the intuitive knowing of our Soul's beauty lead us on to Oneness.

This all points to the potential for conversion, although it hasn't occurred yet. The body is being drawn on by the Soul's desire. The body is converted as well as the mind to the Soul's need when the Mystic Marriage occurs.

Gold is symbolic of the sun, and silver of the moon— sun (masculine), moon (feminine)—and together they symbolize Oneness. Thus the symbol of opposites together draws us on.

VERSES 12, 13

While the king was on his couch,
    my nard gave forth its fragrance.
My beloved is to me a bag of myrrh,
    that lies between my breasts.

One of the reasons that this poem has been interpreted as physical, sexual love between a shepherd and a shepherdess is that so many of the descriptions appeal to our physical senses. The eyes (jewels), the sense of smell (perfume), hearing (music), touch (imagination of lovely garments), tasting (the wine, grape, fruit). It is understandable. However each physical sensation has a parallel spiritual feeling and thus as we seek the esoteric meaning of the poem we interpret the physical as the spiritual.

Perfume (nard) expresses a mind laden with nostalgia and emotion. Certainly as our king (our God) is lying near us, our mind would be infiltrated with emotion and memories of those superior feelings we had at other times.

Nard was a fragrant ointment. Myrrh has several definitions. According to Corinne Heline, it symbolizes a sacred ceremony or the Soul ready for a higher level of consciousness. It sometimes symbolizes the resurrection of the physical to the spiritual. Myrrh between the breasts indicates that the Beloved is close to the feminine symbol (the breasts). Jung suggests that the breasts indicate androgyny. They also symbolize the Divine Mother. So the way is being prepared for the conversion.

VERSE 14

My beloved is to me a cluster of henna blossoms
in the vineyards of Engedi.

The vineyard is related to the perfection that man can produce. The henna blossoms are on a plant the leaves of which are used to make a reddish-orange dye or a brownish-red dye. Engedi represents a fountain. A fountain indicates, from a spiritual sense, the flowing, cleansing life of Spirit.

So what have we here?

I should like to suggest that when one studies the world religions at the esoteric level, many commonalities emerge. The connection between Eastern religions and so-called Western is quite apparent. We have seen the similarity between Christian mysticism and Hindu teaching on the feminine meeting the masculine in Oneness (p. 4). In this verse I believe we are again being reminded of the divine energy, the Kundalini, that will course up the spine as we come closer to Oneness with God.

There are seven chakras in the etheric body, so-called aura of the human body. When these are energized and vibrating at a high frequency and we are totally conscious of the Divinity that we seek, we reach the Mystic Marriage or Enlightened stage. This reference to henna blossoms and a fountain symbolizes the beginning of the opening of the chakras. The color of the first chakra, as seen by clairvoyants, is dark red. The spine is like a fountain. The first chakra lies at the base of the spine.

Verse 14 is referring to the fountain of spirit which flows up the spine to open the chakra centers of the etheric body. (The opening of the chakras is further described in Chapter 7:1-5.) The bride, which is your Soul and mine, is indicating readiness for her conversion. Or, to make it more plain: you and I, in our feminine aspect, are indicating our readiness for a spiritual experience. The feminine is the intuitive, the emotions, the feeling nature. We are ready.

And God calls us on, for it is we who are desired by our Maker.

The masculine calls to the feminine within. God, the Lover, speaks:

VERSES 15-17

Behold, you are beautiful, my love;
 behold, you are beautiful;
 your eyes are doves.
Behold, you are beautiful, my beloved,
 truly lovely.

Our couch is green;
　　the beams of our house are cedar,
　　our rafters are pine.

In these verses we read many comparisons to nature. Nature has always been part of spiritual worship, as throughout nature there is the Presence, and we see It expressed through minerals, plants, animals, birds. There is a silent majesty in trees. At Illumination one is able to perceive the energy, the Light, that is the life of all. Here we are using nature to describe the qualities of the Soul and of God.

The eyes compared to doves brings us a picture of peace, innocence, meekness, quietness. All of these we are as we come to the process of preparing for the Mystical Marriage. The Soul is at rest and the eyes reflect this aspect as a dove reflects it in nature. Peace within the Soul shows forth in the eyes.

All colors have a deep esoteric meaning. The color rays are said to be radiating down to earth at a specific rate of vibration. There is response from us consciously or unconsciously as our eyes observe these colors. There are seven color rays that are basic. Each vibrates at a different rate. From the lowest vibration to the highest some occultists see them thus: red (the lowest) has healing energy; orange, next on the spectrum, is a warm and invigorating vibration. Then occurs yellow, which symbolizes wisdom. Green is in the middle and is between the warm colors and the cooler ones; it is for harmonizing and pacifying. Next we go to the healing colors: blue, indigo, and violet; these are more soothing and healing. Blue is love, devotional harmony; indigo is a soothing color; and violet represents noble spiritual aspiration. As we progress through the book, we will use these colors to interpret passages.

The cedar and the pine, being evergreen, symbolize eternity. Again, green harmonizes and pacifies; it is often assigned to the heart chakra, which is the love chakra—and so the couch is love. The beams of the house are for eternity. "House" symbolizes consciousness. Our inner harmony is necessary as we go toward the moment of conversion. The Betrothal will come as God speaks to us and quiets us.

Our house, our couch, our structure are all getting ready. When we have the experience of realizing our Christ Self, we shall be in a place of harmony and love. Our preparation continues in Chapter 2 of the Song.

Chapter Two of
The Song of Songs

The Bride:

VERSE 1

I am a rose of Sharon,
  a lily of the valleys.

Roses have symbolized high spiritual awareness for
hundreds of years. The Rosicrucians name the seven
chakra centers of the etheric body *roses*. The seven roses
of the cross is their symbol. A rose symbolizes the open
chakra, which is often a sign of completion and perfection.
The lily is an emblem of purity, the Virgin Mary.

Sharon symbolizes harmonious, fruitful, prosperous. So
the rose of Sharon is in its rightful place of high spiritual
awareness. Our Soul is such. We need to recognize it. The
valley is a lower level than the mountains (high spiritual
experience) that surround it. But purity (lily) is in this
lower level also. The Bride is recognizing her high spiritual
awareness and also her final goal of perfection. As we imagine this exalted state, our consciousness is lifted up.

The Bridegroom speaks:

VERSE 2

As a lily among brambles,
   so is my love among maidens.

As we are perceived by God we are seen as complete, perfect, and pure. That is difficult for us to accept, as we have for so long seen ourselves as base, impure, and tainted with earth life. Our religions and our society have helped us see ourselves thus. But in God's eyes we are pure. And the sooner we accept that, the closer we will be to completion.

It is that purity within which we all are that Jesus spoke of: "Blessed are the pure in heart for they shall see God." The pure in heart are those who see themselves, as well as others, as pure. We are in the Age of Aquarius. We are beginning to realize who we are. We are beings of Light, Love, Harmony, Peace, and Joy. So we are getting ready for our great experience by accepting our own Divinity.

Lilies are spoken of several times in the Song. Also in Matthew 6:28, 29 we have Jesus referring to the lilies: "Consider the lilies of the field, how they grow, they neither toil nor spin, yet I tell you, even Solomon in all his glory was not arrayed like one of these." It is interesting that he referred to Solomon and the lily together. But, of course, Jesus knew many books of the Old Testament by memory, it is said. It is quite likely that the Song of Songs was one of them. The lily, the purity of consciousness, is how God sees us.

In Verse 2 the masculine element repeats the element of purity and says that love is pure among all the brambles or thorns of our life. We are pure.

In Verse 3 the Bride-to-be describes the God of the Soul. For we are reminded again and again that our Soul seeks Oneness with our God; thus the opposites, the masculine and the feminine, come together in Oneness, in androgyny. The soul is feminine, God is masculine. Our awareness of God will be complete then. We are God all along—we must accept that.

VERSE 3

As an apple tree among the trees of the wood,
    so is my beloved among young men.
With great delight I sat in his shadow,
    and his fruit was sweet to my taste.

It is because of the need to be at One with the Divine that we look for metaphors that more clearly explain our need for fulfillment. When we speak of apples, most readers go to the apple in the Garden of Eden. But this apple has an opposite quality, for we are moving back into our awareness of our Divinity and not being separated by it as in the fable of the Garden of Eden.

Here the love and adoration the Bride feels for God is being discussed. The Lover offers shade to us when the heat of life becomes too intense.

Now it is not necessary to be at ease in our physical bodies in order to have a conversion. For some it comes when they are in great pain. They then may reach out for help from Him that they do not know. When reaching the Betrothal, they will lose all their pain, and the physical is filled with delight.

In a spiritual sense the apple, a fruit, refers to androgyny. The idea of balance between our two opposites is sweet to our eyes, to our thoughts, to our taste, to our imagination.

The Bride-to-be is comparing her Beloved to other young men. He is as superior as the apple tree is to other trees. She sits in his shadow (shade) which, of course, is so important to one who is living in a place that is uncomfortable. (This Song was written in a desert setting, no doubt.) And the fruit is Love, the sweetest experience we can have.

We have a foretaste of conversion in the following verse:

VERSE 4

He brought me to the banqueting house,
and his banner over me was love.

"He brought me" is so true. It is God that brings us to the banquet for fulfillment of all our needs. He it is who ever follows our progress and our regressions. He it is who knows our needs. Remember that the He referred to is that spark of Divinity within each of us called the Christ by some. It has been with us throughout all our lives, and it knows our real needs. Through Him we are led to the banqueting table. We are not always aware of where we are being led, and we each have our own route. But we go eventually, for that is our spiritual and human need. The banqueting house is our inner place of peace. Our appetites are satisfied there. Enlightenment is our goal and our aspiration.

A banner designates the tribe or group we belong to. His banner is over all of us. His banner floats in the breeze and is Love. How else can we explain God? How can we explain Love? It is Love that we are living for. We all know that subliminally. It is Love we seek. It is Love that heals every dis-ease. It is Love, and His banner is Love.

The Soul within recognizes this and is well on its way to conversion. For when we see our Beloved as our Love, we are "hooked." We all long to be loved and to express love. So often we think that love from other human beings will fill that longing, but usually we are disappointed if we rely on that. It is Universal Love, Pure Love, that we hunger for. And the apple of harmony, beauty, color, and seed for the future symbolizes the beauty of Love. How wonderful to know that His Love is a banner over us!

VERSE 5

Sustain me with raisins,
    refresh me with apples;
    for I am sick with love.

Again, fruits of the spirit are what we long for. The raisin, from the grape, is symbolic of the wine of life. The apple, as has been mentioned, is fruit for the Soul. And so we are begging for more than we have, for we are sick with our longing for Oneness, for Divine Love.

VERSE 6

O that his left hand were under my head,
    and that his right hand embraced me!*

Again, deep longing is expressed. Left and right, the opposites are together and offer a simile for our experience in the spiritual. How important are hands! They serve us and so many others. They touch us with gentleness and anger. They feed us, clothe us, produce our living, and allow us to be creative through art, music, writing, sculpture. We use them to express our most intimate divine knowing, and in love they stroke us, pat us, and carry the feeling of love. The right hand is considered masculine and the left feminine.

In the intimate position described here we know that awareness of the Divine is very near.

---

*This verse is identical with 8:3.

Verse 7

I adjure you, O daughters of Jerusalem,
    by the gazelles or the hinds of the field,
that you stir not up nor awaken love
    until it please.

This is addressed by the feminine or the Soul to the feminine thoughts (daughters) of the old state of consciousness
(Jerusalem) as a warning. For, once we stir up this love, it
will not let us alone. It is daughters of New Jerusalem (a
state of peace and completion) that we are becoming. The
old Jerusalem state of consciousness is being left behind.
If we swear by our animal-like, human nature, we may not
stir up this love. But when we leave that, we stir it up.

It frightens us sometimes to realize where we are being
led. We have flashes of realization of how wonderful it
would be, but we know we shall be leaving behind so
much that is familiar. Especially our old society—daughters of Jerusalem. But once we are awakened, we cannot
go back. And the awakening may come at an instant of
time or through many experiences before we bow our head
and accept our Divinity.

How abstract this poem! No wonder it has been an
enigma to so many. Like the Book of Revelation, it has had
many, many interpretations given from the consciousness
of the writer. Many knew that there was a deep Truth in
it and they were correct in their understanding. For those
of us who are on, or who are seeking, the Mystic Path, it
has the meaning that is coming forth here.

Verse 8

The voice of my beloved!
    Behold, he comes,

leaping upon the mountains,
bounding over the hills.

In our mind's eye we can see this something running to
us. However, this is not a physical consciousness speaking, but a spiritual one. Let us imagine what it means
spiritually.

The voice of my Beloved is that inner soft awareness—
the still point—that does not so much speak as give us feelings of great joy and ecstasy. The voice is silent as the
turtle. The voice is silent but speaks loudly—a paradox,
which most spiritual truths are. It is exciting when we
"hear" it.

He, the Divinity that speaks to us, is a very high level
of consciousness. Mountains symbolize high places of
awareness. We feel, and sometimes see with our physical
eyes, this wonderful Being coming toward us from a higher
state of awareness. He comes swiftly and silently.

VERSE 9

My beloved is like a gazelle,
    or a young stag.
Behold, there he stands
    behind our wall,
gazing in at the windows [heart],
    looking through the lattice.

You see, our Beloved will not intrude until we invite
Him in. We may allow Him to stand outside, gazing into
our heart for many years before we extend the invitation.
He is not shy. He respects our freedom of choice. Freedom
is one of our great gifts that God has allowed us. When we
lose our freedom of choice we are miserable, for it is our

divine right, and God does not impose His Will on us until we open to Him. And then it is our choice whether we follow or not. So the Beloved waits without but may speak to us in hushed tones.

The Bridegroom speaks:

VERSE 10

Arise, my love, my fair one,
    and come away;

What a lovely invitation, and it carries with it an assurance that there is nothing to fear.

VERSE 11

for lo, the winter is past,
    the rain is over and gone.

The cold uncomfortable time has passed. The time of sleeping before the resurrection to new life is in the past. The dreary, dark days of winter have gone. Now is the time of spring and to realize:

VERSE 12

The flowers appear on the earth,
    the time of singing has come,
and the voice of the turtledove
    is heard in our land.

Resurrection time has come.

The flowers of new growth are appearing. The time of festival of song is here. The dove is cooing with its plaintive affection. The time of new growth, blooming, and beauty has come to our earth consciousness. What a won-

derful wooing, and it happens in everyone's consciousness
sooner or later. And the autumn time, of gathering in, is
in the future.

VERSE 13

The fig tree puts forth its figs,
    and the vines are in blossom;
    they give forth fragrance.

Summer is also come. The fruit trees are bearing fruit.
Fruit often refers to the opening of the chakras in our
etheric body, which are affected by our conscious realization of our Divinity and which in turn affect our body and
consciousness. When they are open, they are heavenly
fruit. The vine is sometimes said to refer to the spine, and
the branches to the nerves.

The scent of the blossoms alludes to the beginning of the
opening of the chakras, which will continue to mature until the full ripening, or opening, has been achieved. All is
being prepared for that wonderful moment of conversion
when we are betrothed to our God. He is calling us on!

VERSE 14

O my dove, in the clefts of the rock,
    in the covert of the cliff,
let me see your face,
    let me hear your voice,
for your voice is sweet,
    and your face is comely.

We pretend we have no Soul. Oh, we know there is
something mysterious within us, but we cover up the calling by busy-ness, by duty, by selfish desires, by alcohol,
by drugs (legal and illegal), by sexual activity. We hide

among the rocks of our life. We hide away in the valleys of unhappiness. We deny the existence of this mysterious something. But God continues to call us out, to call us to come out, for He knows we are each beautiful, with a sweetly vibrating voice and with a face that is lovely. So often when we ignore our Divinity we have no self-esteem. Self-esteem can be built on affairs of the world and being successful, but it will eventually crash. True self-esteem is Self-Awareness of how Godlike we really are. The dove is the Holy Spirit, our Holy Spirit, the Breath of Life, the Soul.

God is calling us from the secret recesses of our thoughts and feelings. He wants us to recognize our own wonder.

VERSE 15

Catch us the foxes,
　　the little foxes,
that spoil the vineyard,
　　for our vineyards are in blossom.

Animals in dreams symbolize instincts from the unconscious. It is that which often keeps us from expressing or realizing our own Divine Being. The fox is considered stealthy and often steals. However, our deep need may overcome or catch these instincts and will not allow them to spoil the vineyard by eating our blossoming awareness of God. And God is outside our window, calling us on. We catch the foxes so they cannot spoil the beginning of our awareness, our blossoms, which will mature into fruit and, eventually, the Wine of Life.

In Verses 16 and 17 we capitulate. It happens in a flash, in a second of man's time. It needs little description, for when we experience it, we *know* without need of words.

VERSES 16, 17

My beloved is mine and I am his,
    he pastures his flock among the lilies.
Until the day breathes
    and the shadows flee,
turn, my beloved, be like a gazelle,
    or a young stag upon rugged mountains.

We feel in this experience that there are only our own Soul and God present. We are entirely alone. No other human being is part of the experience. The Beloved is truly all ours. It is our very Soul in that instant. For a brief moment we are One. All opposites have flown away. All is right with the world. We have reached a high moment of certainty. "My beloved is mine and I am his." He is ever-present. The lily being a perfect beauty of purity is where our God thoughts (flocks) will now pasture. We are lifted up to such a high level of consciousness and we beg him to stay with us forever or at least until the day breaks and we have to go back to our duties.

The gazelle and young stag move with swiftness and freedom. So it is as our God awareness comes to us, for we feel completely free for the first time in our life. We are truly loved and we have this divine knowing to take with us forever.

At this experience one is converted. The experience has been beyond anything known in the physical. The aspirant may have such a high ecstasy throughout the body and conscious awareness that it can only be compared to a sexual orgasm. But it is so much more, so much more. It is the masculine and feminine, it is God and the Soul, coming together within conscious awareness for a brief time in purity and beauty and love.

Now some interpret this experience as "I am saved," "I have known God," "I am born again." Paul experienced on the road to Damascus the great white light and the "voice" of Jesus speaking to him. He was blind and ill for three days. It took him many years subsequent to that experience to fully appreciate the experience of Jesus speaking to him, which was his conversion. He had much suffering and work before he finally accepted his Mystic Path. So it is with most of us. We never forget the experience, but we may put it on the back burner until another, more propitious, time. But we will never be the same. It is only the beginning.

It is often true that after conversion we somehow allow the physical life and its attendant problems to dim this Light. Although it may remain in our memory, it loses some of its specialness with the coming and going of our daily life experiences. It is a beginning, never to be forgotten, but much more devotion to the Path is required before we reach the next experience, the Marriage.

After my conversion, I went through many years of pain and psychological upset. I took many wrong turns. I went to the bottom of guilt and sorrow. I still depended on my own intellect and logical thinking. Throughout that time, however, there was the memory of that Light experience, and of course the Silent Love of That was ever with me. I dreamed of a knight on a white horse coming to rescue me. (He had already come, but I did not recognize Him.) It was not until I lost a son in the Vietnam War that I took my next step. I knew that the Light Being was with me.

This was the turning point. Then it was I knew I had been rejecting God. Then it was I knew I had to leave the desires and attachments of the personal life and turn to Universal Love and Life. Now God did not *bring* this sorrow, but God *gathered* these sorrows and made them into the opposite, the preservation of my life and the joy of giving spiritual food to others spiced with sweet-smelling and sweet-tasting spices. My story continues:

Before hearing from the army sergeant about the "death" of my son, I had a precognitive dream that had much the same effect upon me as the first conversion experience. It had a luminous quality lasting a long time, especially during the first week after the news was delivered and we were waiting for his body to be shipped from Vietnam. The dream was as follows:

I was divorced from my husband (which I was legally) and occupying an apartment. My ex-husband had taken our three children to the movies. It was very late at night and I wondered why they had not returned. Then he brought the little boy home—in the dream he was about four years old—and took the two girls to spend the night with him. I wanted to undress my son and put him to bed, but, true to his personality, he stubbornly resisted. He was dressed in navy blue shorts and shirt. He went into the back yard and sat on a rock. I watched through the window. One arm was behind his back. A butterfly landed on that arm and it tickled him. He moved the arm, the butterfly flew up, and he tried to catch it but failed. Then the sun rose in the East. He said, "What a beautiful sunset." I did not correct him, but I knew it was a sunrise. Then I brought him into the house to his bedroom and undressed him. There was a knock on the door. I was alarmed, picked him up, and went to the front door. I could see a uniform cap on the man standing outside but was unafraid, as the door was locked. The little boy was asleep by then. As I said to myself, "We are safe," I heard the stranger's key turning in the lock.

Twenty-four hours later I received the message.

This was a second conversion. You see, God is patient and is waiting for us to turn to Him. Death, disaster, loss of possessions and relationships are the times when we are most open to His advances. All during that week, waiting for his body and for the funeral, I was guided and I felt calm and sure that all was well. I had had the Vision and was reminded that I had once been chosen and was being guided again.

From that time I began my sincere search and had no idea where it would lead me, for I was unaware of the metaphysical movement, the transcendentalists, the mystics, the belief in the Christ within. But I was guided step by step on my Path. Meditation was the next step.

Out of this experience I was turned to the study of world religions, Jungian psychology, dream interpretation, and the Bible—and to worldwide travel to gain firsthand knowledge of religions and people. I became aware of the need for growth in consciousness through meditation and contemplation and then began writing books. I am not finished, but I am on my way. Or as is said, "God is not finished with me yet."

In our next section we shall discuss meditation, concentration, contemplation. After the initial experience there is much work to be done before we reach that goal of the Mystic Marriage, or, if you prefer, the Divine Union, and confirmation in the life of a mystic.

Chapter Three of
The Song of Songs

Before we continue with our interpretation of the Song, I should like to give an overview of meditation.

But first I must point out that the four steps I am following, i.e. Conversion—Betrothal; Contemplation or Meditation—Marriage; Mystical Marriage—Union with God; Fruitfulness and Service; may not be experienced in the same order by every aspirant. Some people may start with meditation. Many are seeking they know not what through various meditative techniques. As a result, the conversion may come second or the mystical experience might occur first and guide the beginner into closer contact through meditation. One does not know how much of this ground has been covered in a former life and thus each of us may be further along than we realize. But for convenience, and because this is the order followed by many mystics, I shall follow the four steps given.

We can be sure of one thing, we cannot force any of these to occur. All come by the Grace of the Spirit, and if we consciously decide it is time to have the experience of the Spiritual Marriage, we may drive it away. Most mystics testify that they are greatly surprised when they have the experience. When we are ready it will occur. Sometimes, the high energy-level experienced could not be tolerated by our physical body. And so we must do what we know will lead us on and not have any "great expectation" of where or when, or of immediate fulfillment. It will happen eventually in this life or another, and we will know when it has happened, without doubt!

Meditation—the art of—comes out of Eastern teaching. As we've noted, Western organized religion was suspicious of it and felt that the masses were not ready for it. Indeed, the monks were ordered not to practice it in the early days of the Catholic church. Meditation is occasionally practiced in the Catholic church now, although not institutionalized. Also meditation tends to make a person independent and resistant to the edicts of the church. The Protestant church has not taught it either although many are doing so now. For these reasons and others we had to turn to the East to learn about it.

We have had many fine teachers coming to us from India, Japan, and China as well as Korea to teach us. This has brought the two, East and West, together and has made us closer to being One World. However, there are millions of people in the West who still follow the traditional teachings of prayer and doing what their Soul needs. They are where they should be. Prayer is important at all stages of development, but meditation becomes most important when we step on the Mystic Path. Prayer is usually addressed outward to a Being that is outside of our inner consciousness. Meditation is defined as the stopping of thoughts and focusing on an Inner Self and listening for guidance.

There are many methods taught by Eastern and Western "gurus." I feel that it behooves us to follow a more Western type, because we do not have the Oriental mind or inheritance of close association with the unconscious mind. Clearly we have been very centered in the conscious mind while the religions of the East more often have been in the unconscious.

Bringing together the conscious and the unconscious is one of the main results of meditation and a necessary step before we can have the numinous experience of the Mystic Marriage.

There are other methods of bringing our conscious awareness of our Christ forth, to marry the conscious and unconscious: dream interpretation, study and practice of the tenets of Jungian psychology, methods of therapy by psychologists of other schools and persuasions, and commitment to our Path. Help from a psychologist, however, is not absolutely vital. Many of us are able, by using denials and affirmations, to clear our unconscious so the Light of the Soul can shine into our conscious mind. Dedication, prayer, meditation, study can do wonders.

I prefer presenting here a description of meditation based on Western philosophy—although it also has Eastern overtones, as all meditation is primarily Eastern. Vera Stanley Alder in *The Finding of the Third Eye* is the source of this sequence. However, again, being individual in this activity, you may not follow these in the order given; or you may skip some of the steps; or you may have an entirely different way of describing your experience.

She talks about four steps: concentration, meditation, contemplation, and adoration.

Concentration follows relaxation of the body. It is focusing attention on an object, the breath, a thought, music. Its aim is to stop the thoughts from skittering from one idea to another. Since the conscious mind must be at rest, we may concentrate on one thought such as a mantra. This will eventually be unnecessary as one learns to go into the Silence immediately.

Meditation proper then follows. This is when we allow the unconscious intuitive mind to function. We may take a question and focus on it, waiting for an answer. We may choose an object, an idea, a subject and allow the intuitive to feed us some idea. Now the conscious mind is active, and often we may want to record our ideas through writing, painting, composing music. We are releasing the Inner Knowledge. To do this well may require the seeker to meditate for years. Be patient. True education is releasing this inner knowledge. Religious ideas may come forth at this time and become creativity. Einstein is said to have received many of his ideas while walking and meditating. By the way, walking meditation, jogging, or skiing meditation is often the best method for the active person.

You will begin to *know* the Truth rather than believe in it.

Sometimes you may tap the collective unconscious as well as the personal unconscious. This may bring to your conscious mind wonderful ideas.

Contemplation is at a deeper level although the dividing line is often blurred. This is a deep level of knowing. The cause, the inner meaning, the law behind a quality comes to awareness. The intellect is quiet. Words are not needed. Deep listening is required. The answer may come in the form of a feeling, a fleeting word, a knowing, an unsought thought, without your knowing how you know. It is too abstract to describe. Creativity also comes from this phase but is truly strange to the conscious mind. Poetry, painting, composition of music may result. It is too noetic to describe. But you will know when it happens.

Adoration naturally follows—for meditation and contemplation will take one into the deepest gratitude. The results are often of such ecstatic feeling that one can hardly contain it. And each naturally turns to praise and thanks-giving for the love that is engendered during this period. At this point we *know* God.

Adoration and love are synonymous. At once one is in Unity with All. Oneness is achieved. All is feeling—no words can describe. And out of this may come the experience of the Mystic Marriage.

My meditation experience began after I went through what I call a psychic phase. Many aspirants become very interested in astrology, numerology, spiritualism, guidance by a psychic before they learn to meditate and to be guided by their Inner Spirit. Eventually I realized that I needed to study and to meditate in order to understand my Path. I never thought of being a mystic. I just knew that I was being guided down a path that was right for me. It takes commitment and discipline to do this alone. A group or a teacher helps many start the process of meditation. Many fine books helped me. Eventually I found a group.

Let us now turn to Chapter 3 of the Song of Songs. The bride speaks.

VERSE 1

Upon my bed by night
    I sought him whom my soul loves;
I sought him, but found him not;
    I called him, but he gave no answer.

This is referring to meditation. Sleep, dreaming, bed all refer to the state of meditation. So in the quiet of the dark night, when the cares of the day are stopped, our Soul seeks God. But we may not find Him, for it takes much more than getting quiet. And we may give up and allow our thoughts to wander.

VERSE 2

"I will rise now and go about the city,
  in the streets and in the squares;
I will seek him whom my soul loves."
  I sought him, but found him not.

And so when we are not successful, we let our thoughts
wander. We go to the outside thoughts, to the world, to the
conscious thoughts. We will not find the deep touch with
Him there, for the city (many thoughts) is wrapped up in
the physical. However, we long for this union. We do not
find it either in books, education, lectures, church, or
representatives of the church. Only in our Innner
Awareness.

VERSE 3

The watchmen found me,
  as they went about in the city.
"Have you seen him whom my soul loves?"

Interesting that the Bride should say "whom my soul
loves." It is our Soul that longs for God. We have body,
mind, emotions, and Soul. (Soul is used here as meaning
our individual spirit.) The Soul ever longs for reunion with
God.
The watchmen do not know about God in this deep
sense but may guide us. The watchmen are conscious
thoughts.

VERSE 4

Scarcely had I passed them,
  when I found him whom my soul loves.

When the aspirant passes the conscious thoughts, lets them go, then God is found. It is in the depths of the Soul that we find God. It is the Marriage of our Soul and God that we seek. It is unification.

VERSE 4 (cont'd)

I held him, and would not let him go
    until I had brought him into my mother's
        house,
        and into the chamber of her that
            conceived me.

The feminine in our psyche is the Soul. The feminine is the daughter, the mother, the wife. So when we finally make contact, it is as though we had opened our feminine (mother) consciousness (house) to Him and allowed Him to enter. It is in the realm (chamber) of the feminine that our desire for God is conceived.

In understanding the experience we have in meditation, we can treat it like a dream (both come from the unconscious), and the unconscious reveals itself in symbols. So these verses are interpreted from symbolic position.

VERSE 5

I adjure you, O daughters of Jerusalem,
    by the gazelles or the hinds of the field,
    that you stir not up nor awaken love
        until it please.

Verse five is like Chapter 2:7 and 8:4. It refers to the old feminine consciousness (daughters of Jerusalem) being warned not to waken this great awareness of love until the right time. Most of the emotions we feel in meditation are love, joy, ecstasy, peace. The old consciousness may not understand this.

Now we go into a very abstract concept—a description of the meditation experience. This could be classified in the division designated as contemplation. It is at a deeper level and very symbolic. Any time we try to describe our experience on the contemplative level, we can be misunderstood. But we shall try.

VERSE 6

What is that coming up from the wilderness,
    like a column of smoke,
perfumed with myrrh and frankincense,
    with all the fragrant powders of the
        merchant?

The wilderness is a lower state of consciousness. In the Bible it is often used to indicate a confused state, two examples being Moses and Jesus in the wilderness. Both had experiences in the wilderness after their conversion. This state is seeming chaos, but all experiences have a foundation in God. Our world is God's world. Our planet is impregnated with God's essence. It is this essence that seems to be ethereal smoke. But when it comes closer, we see it as beautiful and filled with qualities that appeal to our senses. This is another way of describing how wonderful the experience is.

Here I must discuss another evolutionary step. I have touched on this previously.

We not only have a physical body, but according to esotericists we have an astral body, which is our emotions, and a mental body, and a spirit body called *etheric*. All of these become unified when we evolve to the Mystic Marriage stage. All are spiritualized. They then are raised to consciousness of Oneness with the spiritual body, and that Oneness is Divine. They all merge, and the physical body is transformed into pure white light in this process. That is the reason the Hindu has explained the transformation of the physical by teaching the concept of the Divine Energy that opens the chakras in the etheric body that are attached to the endocrine glands of the physical body. When these are opened and whirling at a high energy rate, the physical becomes pure light.*

Now back to our Verse 6. Myrrh has many meanings. It is thought by some to symbolize the Soul body, and frankincense the physical body. When these are fully filled with the Higher Energies, they are compared to perfume. It is said that an enlightened one has a lovely perfume issuing from him/her.

From another mystic, Charles Fillmore, we have frankincense as symbolizing the transmutation of the physical to the spiritual, and myrrh symbolizing resurrection. Thus the perfume arising from these indicates the high level of the scene being depicted. All are a part of the Godhead.

VERSE 7

Behold, it is the litter of Solomon!

This is a vision coming to the meditator. When in deep meditation or the stage of contemplation we may have visions, we may have active imagination, which is Jung's term for inner conversation with a figure that appears, or

---

*There are different explanations of the various bodies by other esotericists.

just a conversation or experience with our Inner Self. This is often understood as coming from the intuitive level.

We have used Solomon as symbolic of God. So the Soul is seeing a pageant relating to her experience of that time. We explain our visions in terms of present experience.

VERSES 7 (cont'd), 8

About it are sixty mighty men
    of the mighty men of Israel,
        [*spiritual consciousness*]
all girt with swords
    and expert in war,
each with his sword at his thigh,
    against alarms by night.

In our mind's eye we can see this array of men with swords buckled on close to the center of power. They also surround the litter. It is a powerful scene.

VERSES 9, 10

King Solomon made himself a palanquin [*throne*]
    from the wood of Lebanon [*pure thoughts*].
He made its posts of silver [*feminine*],
        its back of gold [*masculine*], its seat of purple [*the*
        color that has the highest vibration];
it was lovingly wrought within
    by the daughters of Jerusalem.

Again a description of the high state of adoration that comes to us in meditation. The King, God the Father, is on a throne of pure thoughts, with the masculine and feminine balanced and with the royal color supporting It. It lovingly comes to us by our spiritual thoughts, albeit of an older dispensation (daughters of Jerusalem) which will pass away as we reach the New Jerusalem state of consciousness. But this is our description as we start on our path. The palanquin may refer to our Light body or Soul, which is beyond all physical destruction. The cedars of Lebanon, it is said, cannot be burned. God weaves this garment for us and it is most precious.

VERSE 11

Go forth, O daughters of Zion,

Zion was considered to be Jerusalem but sometimes used as a figure for the New Jerusalem. New Jerusalem is spiritual consciousness, a new state of divine awareness.

VERSE 11 (cont'd)

and behold King Solomon,
with the crown with which his mother
crowned him
on the day of his wedding,
on the day of the gladness of his heart.

We can understand how it was possible for many interpreters of this Song to see this verse as a description of the procession of the Bridegroom coming to the wedding. But for our purpose we have understood the Bridegroom to be God, Universal Spirit, and the Bride to be our individual Soul, the spirit within. We are "seeing" this or imagining it in meditation. It leads us upward.

As we look at the scene, we see the balance between the opposites (gold and silver)—the royal nature of the throne. And the throne is the seventh chakra at the crown of the head. That is often called the throne of the Most High, and the color is purple (violet).

The Hindu teaching is that the Divine Energy, the Kundalini Power, courses up the spine (column of smoke), opens the six chakras (6 chakras, which in numerology is 60 reduced) which are clothed with Truth, and finally meets the Shakti at the crown of the head, which is defined as All Being, Pure Knowing, All Truth. This is called Samadhi, Enlightenment. The Catholic mystics call it the Mystic Marriage.

Verse 11 seems to describe the final step which we see in a vision and will experience sometime on our journey in the Spiritual seeking. It calls us on.

"Go forth, O daughters of Zion" is referring to the high feminine consciousness of the New Jerusalem as the Kingdom of Heaven so often referred to by Jesus.

"And behold King Solomon with the crown," etc.: what the meditator is experiencing is a vision of him/her self crowned as the King, for we are all King or God—we merely need to open up our consciousness to this Truth. The mother is crowning us as King, as the feminine energy that becomes one with the masculine. Our wedding brings together the Mother/Father God of us all.

And such Joy reigns!

Meditation, contemplation, gives us this glimpse of Reality.

We will continue with our journey of meditation in Chapter 4 of the Song. There our Lover, God, speaks to us.

Chapter Four of
The Song of Songs

The inner conversation we develop with our higher awareness of Spirit is an important part of meditation. It is listening to guidance from our unconscious. We know it will guide us into more joy, more fruitfulness, and the right service. It is the source of intuition, of creativity, of awareness of who we really are. It is one of the more important results of meditation, for it leads us on our evolutionary journey.

God woos us. Oh, it may be on an unconscious level, but He is forever calling us to Him. It is natural, for we have left His Presence and are stumbling along, eating of the husks with the pigs—as the story of the prodigal son relates. But all the time, our memory of our former Oneness with all Divinity speaks to us. As a result, we are restless and never quite satisfied. And God continues to woo us.

In this chapter we have a response from Him whom we seek. As we meditate, we have experiences that lift us up to the highest ecstasy. And still we are not at the Mystic Wedding. This feeling of being perfect, of being accepted, of being loved by God is an important phase of our meditation and is called a marriage, but not the Mystic Marriage.

This chapter indeed sounds like a lover making love to his Bride. For it is filled with allusions to her perfection. We are perfect but have not recognized it yet. We are perfect, and here our Inner Voice is telling us so.

As we would expect, there is much that is symbolic in this chapter. After all, this is coming from the deep level of the unconscious and, as we've noted, it is only through symbolism that it can be expressed. God "speaks" in all languages from the common language of symbols. He speaks to us personally, and He speaks to the entire human race.

VERSES 1–5

Behold, you are beautiful, my love,
    behold, you are beautiful!
Your eyes are doves
    behind your veil.
Your hair is like a flock of goats,
    moving down the slopes of Gilead.
Your teeth are like a flock of shorn ewes
    that have come up from the washing,
all of which bear twins,
    and not one among them is bereaved.
Your lips are like a scarlet thread,
    and your mouth is lovely.
Your cheeks are like halves of a pomegranate
    behind your veil.
Your neck is like the tower of David,
    built for an arsenal,
whereon hang a thousand bucklers,
    all of the shields of warriors.
Your two breasts are like two fawns,
    twins of a gazelle,
        that feed among the lilies.

Verses 1–5 contain symbolic language such as dove (higher aspect of love); goats (eternal life); Gilead (high consciousness that endures); ewes that are white and healthy without sorrow (thoughts that are positive); pomegranate (good works); tower of David (love); gazelle that feeds among the lilies (swift integration of the pure in the unconscious).

So what do we have here?

As we meditate, we come to realize our perfection. We are no longer bowed down by our imperfection, for we get the feeling time and time again that we are perfect. Not perfect as the world describes perfection, but perfect as our Spirit is perfect. There is no egotism in this realization. It has nothing to do with what we have caused to happen. It is perfection and beauty that come from within our unconscious. If we are to have the Mystic Marriage, we must believe at some point that we are ready for it. No, not believe, but *know* that we are ready.

Now the feeling of perfection may be a fleeting experience, but it will return time after time until we are ready to accept it. It is not our Inner Soul that denies it, it is our outer personality, our intellect, our analytical, judgmental mind. It is not in the outer but in the Inner.

Being yet more aware of our physical body than of our Soul body, we may see this description as of physical beauty. But looking at the meaning through symbology we get: you are a higher aspect of love; you have eternal life; you have a high consciousness of your Divinity; you are positive in your thoughts; you do good works; and the integration of the good in your unconscious will come swiftly.

Now this is being addressed, let us not forget, to the Soul—the feminine aspect of our Self, the Spirit within. We are being reminded of the Truth that lies in our Soul.

For the Soul is all of these and more. To become aware of it is our conscious Journey.

VERSE 6

Until the day breathes
and the shadows flee,
I will hie me to the mountain of myrrh
and the hill of frankincense.

It is the mountain of myrrh and the hill of frankincense that we seek. Myrrh and frankincense were used in holy ceremonies in holy places. It is a place of consciousness of our Divinity. It is where the God of our Being comes from. It is holy, and when the dawn breaks, when the morning breezes blow, we will be aware of this high and holy place, and all shadows of sorrow, guilt, resentment, negativity will flee. For all is One on this high mountain.

VERSE 7

You are all fair, my love;
there is no flaw in you.

"There is no flaw in you." Have you ever heard that about yourself—either from your own assessment or from others? The Self has no flaws. The Soul is perfect and the Soul is who you really are. Keep in touch with that Soul and have perfect self-esteem. God knows your perfection and God is Perfect. And God loves your Soul.

VERSE 8

Come with me from Lebanon, my bride; . . .
Depart from the peak of Amana [*a high place in consciousness*],

from the peak of Senir [*the Truth that generation
    must be put away for regeneration*] and
    Hermon [*a sublime state of mind*],
from the dens of lions,
    from the mountains of leopards.

The instruction, the plea, from God is that we come
from the highest thoughts (Lebanon) to be One with Him.
Verse 8 is one of the most difficult to fit into this interpretation. However, it seems to me that the Bridegroom, God, is saying to the Soul that there is a higher
place than the physical place, and it symbolizes spiritual
thoughts, regeneration, a sublime state of mind. For in
these places can lurk lions (beauty and fighting spirit) and
leopards (primitive unconscious area of the psyche). It is
difficult for me to picture a higher state of Being, and yet
we know God is above all of these feeble attempts of
mankind to explain His Regency. His Place is beyond
human comprehension, but we will be there when the
Spiritual Marriage occurs.

Now this is all very abstract, but I warned you that all
of this great Song is abstract, and I am trying to put it into
an almost foreign dress by reducing it to words and general
concepts.

In any case, the Bridegroom, God, continues to call us
on. The higher awareness of who we really are continues
to nudge us. And only through meditation and contemplation, deep contact with His Essence, can we get these
flashes of Light.

You see, God wants us as much as we want Him. We
left our Divine Home of Oneness with Him (banishment
from the Garden of Eden legend), and He continues to call
us. He loves us beyond all of our ability to recognize it. A
love that is Pure, Universal. A love that forgives all—even

our lack of attention to Him for years and perhaps many lifetimes. He loves us!

And the Bridegroom says:

VERSE 9

You have ravished my heart . . . with
a glance of your eyes,
with one jewel of your necklace.

One glance from us brings quick response from Him who is waiting.

The use of "my sister, my bride" (next verse) has been suggested as indicative of the closeness of the Song to Egyptian poetry. In Egypt during pharaonic times, the bride of the Pharaoh was his sister. So this simile is understood.

VERSE 10

How sweet is your love, my sister,
my bride!
how much better is your love than wine,
and the fragrance of your oils than
any spice!

Remember what age this was written in when wine, oil, and spice are mentioned. All of these were very important symbols of pleasure for the senses. Oh, how difficult it is for us to accept this! We are so conditioned by our sensual life to believe that the perfume, the bath oil that makes us beautiful, the cosmetics that are used to make us attractive and to attract the opposite sex are most important. But here we are told that love for God is far above all of these. When we say we love these physical cosmetics, we are speaking of a lower level of love. The Divine Love which

we are being called to experience is far above the love of
sense pleasure.

VERSE 11

Your lips distill nectar, my bride;
    honey and milk are under your tongue;
    the scent of your garments is like
        the scent of Lebanon.

Garments refer to the Light body that develops as we
reach this high state. Lebanon: white, clean, pure, high
thoughts.

We should keep in mind that we are at a very high level
of awareness of our Divinity and are being wooed. After all,
the Bride is just waiting for the Marriage. It is the next step
for the Bride, the Soul.

Corinne Heline defines milk and honey as feminine
(milk) and masculine (honey) in each of us. The Promised
Land was referred to as the land of milk and honey. When
these two polarities have come together in consciousness,
we are ready to enter that high state of consciousness
called the Promised Land. This will happen to all of us
eventually. The Promised Land in Jesus' teaching is the
Kingdom of Heaven.

Throughout the Book of Revelation we are reminded of
the Path we shall tread in order to reach the New Jerusalem, or the Kingdom of Heaven. The ups and downs, the
triumphs, the glimpses of the throne all lead us to realize
that the Wedding is going to happen to each of us, eventually. (See my book *Revelation: For a New Age*.)

When the masculine and feminine are One within us,
we experience the Mystic Marriage. Now this is highly important, and our work toward this androgynous state is
primary. As we are guided more and more by the God of

our Being, we balance these opposites. Women learn to express the positive masculine and men learn to express the positive feminine. As they do so they will become unified, and the need for a physical mate will pass. To force this, however, is not Truth. Slowly we allow this to happen. The more we center on God the quicker it occurs, for God is male/female. According to Genesis, we were created in His Image. So we are returning to conscious awareness of our Being.

VERSE 12

A garden locked is my sister, my bride,
a garden locked, a fountain sealed.

The garden refers to the Soul, it is an image of the Soul. It contains the potential of beauty, fruitfulness, completion. But our Soul is locked up many times, and God cannot touch us in the deep recesses of our unconscious—at least we are not consciously aware of Him. The fountain of the "water of life" that Jesus referred to is sealed. It does not flow into our conscious awareness. We are as a virgin, pure and sweet, but locked away from the Bridegroom. We are approaching our Oneness but still resist. We are getting closer through contemplation.

By way of explanation of the relationship of the conscious, unconscious, superconscious, I should like to suggest that the three are in the Mind. The unconscious lies between the conscious and the superconscious. Until the unconscious is cleansed of blocks and shadows, we are not conscious of the superconscious or the Soul which is the spark of God. Consciousness is thus defined as conscious awareness of our God, and the Mystic Marriage celebrates this. I have not based this on any particular psychological theory but have given it as a means of explanation.

VERSE 13

Your shoots are an orchard of pomegranates
with all choicest fruits,
henna with nard,

Our potential is fruitfulness of the Spirit. And fruitfulness comes after the Mystic Marriage. The potential is present. We need to awaken to it.

Using nature as a means of description of our potential is appropriate. The cycles of life are portrayed in nature. The qualities of a higher world are shown. It is a mode of the Infinite.

The pomegranate symbolizes the lure of the sense life, generation, and is good as it often brings us to the realization of regeneration, the transformation of the physical to the spiritual.

VERSES 14, 15

nard and saffron, calamus and cinnamon,
with all trees of frankincense,
myrrh and aloes,
with all chief spices—
a garden fountain, a well of living water,
and flowing streams from Lebanon.

Henna and nard have already been discussed as well as frankincense and myrrh.

And then we have "a garden fountain, a well of living water, and flowing streams from Lebanon." Lebanon is white, brilliant, pure thoughts. The fountain that brings forth living water which Jesus spoke of to the Samaritan woman at the well comes from pure thoughts. Our garden, our Soul, is often overgrown with impure thoughts and is locked in by sensual thoughts. Our task is to purify our thoughts, to live from a positive approach, to learn to affirm the beautiful. Pure, shining thoughts will release the living water from the fountain. Jesus said that living water would allow the person to have eternal life and to thirst no more (John 4: 7–42). It is the living water that we seek unconsciously, as all of us want eternal life.

So we have this great potential waiting to be tapped. God is telling us how beautiful we are. God is pointing out our potential fruitfulness. God is offering us eternal life. What are we waiting for?

The Bride replies:

VERSE 16

Awake, O north wind,
    and come, O south wind!
Blow upon my garden,
    let its fragrance be wafted abroad.
Let my beloved come to his garden,
    and eat its choicest fruits.

Wind is connected with the primary element, the creative breath, or exhalation. It is taken for "breath" or "spirit." At the height of its activity, the wind in a hurricane, it combines the four Elements: air, earth, fire, and water. Thus it is a symbol for fecundation and regeneration. Regeneration is our goal, regeneration of the physical to the spiritual or pure Light. North and South are opposite poles and when brought together are a symbol of Oneness of the opposites.

The Bride capitulates! The Bride calls for the Bridegroom to come to her garden so that the fragrance would be sensed by the whole world. She expresses her adoration.

And she invites her Beloved to come in and eat its choicest fruits. She is ready. But she has not reached the final pinnacle. Doubt from the ego delays the consummation of the Marriage.

The experience of the Mystic Marriage may come to an initiate many times before he/she is ready to give up all attachments, all centeredness in the physical life. The commitment may not be there.

In Chapter 5 we will be reminded of our lack of deep commitment to the course, and as the "Dark Night of the Soul" is experienced, it may take many years or many lives to convince us that the Marriage is our goal and that it is worth all creative suffering. But we will learn from the suffering, for it is part of our evolutionary journey to Enlightenment.

Chapter Five of
The Song of Songs

I come to my garden, my sister, my
    bride.
    I gather my myrrh with my spice,
    I eat my honeycomb with my
        honey,
    I drink my wine with my milk.
Eat, O friends, and drink:
    drink deeply, O lovers!

The Bridegroom, God, comes to our garden, which is not
really our garden but God's garden. For it is divine consciousness which is our Soul. In our thoughts we are
locked, but God comes forth and taps our Inner Spark, our
Soul. Although we have had one experience of Oneness,
we may not be ready to let go of our physical attachments
completely.

Myrrh, as we have noted, is bitter, but with a lovely
odor. It is the experience of life that brings sorrow instead
of joy. The results, when handled in a positive way, can
be pure pleasure, for spices not only were used to embalm
the body of the dead but to enhance the flavor of food for
the living.

The Bridegroom came to the garden, to His garden, in

our Song. Eating honeycomb with honey seems to mean
that all sweetness is being experienced. We have already
observed that honey is often seen as masculine, while milk
symbolizes the feminine. These two together indicate the
nature of the Bridegroom, of God. God is neither male nor
female but fully One with no division.

In this verse the Bridegroom eats honey and drinks milk
and wine. Wine, of course, relates to the living water,
which is the spiritual essence of everything. So the
spiritual essence, combined with milk and honey, brings
forth the experience of the Sacred Marriage. God is offering this metaphor to the Soul, to our Soul, to paint a picture of the result if we let Him in. But He is in the garden,
the outer court of our house, our consciousness. We are
aware of Him and will hear His knocking: "Behold I stand
at the door and knock."

"Eat O friends and drink, drink deeply, O lovers."

Eat of this Truth, drink of this Truth, for we are all
lovers. We are all made in love, seeking love, and using our
time on earth to find our love. And at the deepest level it
is God who is our Lover, the only real Lover we shall ever
have.

Now we are addressed by the Bride. Unconsciously,
perhaps in meditation, she is aware of the love at her door.

VERSE 2

I slept but my heart was awake.

In meditation our heart is awake. The heart is symbolic
of that intuition of love that comes to meet us in meditation. Love is knocking at the door of the heart.

VERSE 2 (cont'd)

Hark! my beloved is knocking.

Universal Love speaks:

"Open to me, my sister, my love,
    my dove, my perfect one;

When we realize that a feminine characteristic is Love,
we can see that both men and women have this experience.
Our heart is always pure. Our Soul is always pure. It may
be encrusted with the results of ignoring it, of not polish-
ing it, but it is pure. And so are we, for we are really only
our Soul.

VERSE 2 (cont'd)
for my head is wet with dew,
    my locks with the drops of the night."

This has been given various interpretations. For me, it
is a phrase that our thoughts might bring as our God tries
to get our attention. The dew is white. This is a Vision of
Light, of a higher Being, coming to us. God is, so to speak,
"left out in the cold" when we do not welcome Him in.
The night is the dark side of our consciousness and seems
to have no Light in it. He is there.

VERSE 3
I had put off my garment,
    how could I put it on?
I had bathed my feet,
    how could I soil them?

She hesitated. The Soul hesitated. The heart hesitated.
Why? Because of laziness, because of attention to physical details, because of fear, because the Bride was unsure
of her desire. A woman whose lover calls to her to open the

door gives no thought to how she should get there. She arises with a bound and lets him in.

In meditation, as we hear this divine request, we may use any excuse not to open to full awareness of the Presence. We have been taught by some religions, by psychology, by race consciousness not to have this one-to-one relationship with God. We have been told it is abnormal. Many psychologists say that the mystic experience is a form of schizophrenia. Intellectual reasoning has become such a part of our belief that we use every conscious or unconscious excuse not to open fully to God. The mystic is not split (schizophrenic) but unified.

There are so many examples of the great wonder and glory and happiness and harmony that come to one who has this close relationship to the Christ within. No longer can we be diverted by those ''experts'' who speak from the intellect alone. We have many witnesses and testimonies to the contrary. The mystic experience is hard to understand intellectually and will probably never be so understood. But fear not; if your centering is on the Good, the True, the Beautiful, you are on the right Path.

To put a garment on symbolizes covering up the Truth. To soil the feet is to distort our understanding. And so we hesitate. This may happen many times as we meditate, contemplate, and are almost there. And then fear from the past, worry about the future enters in, and we do not open to His Love, His Presence.

VERSE 4

My beloved put his hand to the latch,
    and my heart was thrilled within me.

And what a thrill it is! The high ecstasy of the touch of His Love on our love is pure bliss. The heart thrills beyond description. And our reticence is overcome. We spring up to open the door.

VERSE 5

> I arose to open to my beloved,
>> and my hands dripped with myrrh,
> my fingers with liquid myrrh,
>> upon the handles of the bolt.

Perhaps the duality of the Seeker caused these laggard ways. Perhaps before opening the "bolt of the door" the aspirant was not fully convinced. Perhaps that was why the dark night came upon him/her.

The Good News Bible reads of Verse 4: My lover put his hand to the door/And I was thrilled that he was near.

The door to our heart is there. It can be reached and touched by God. But it cannot be opened by God. Only the Bride, our Soul, can open from the inside. We may feel a deep thrill as God touches this latch through His Grace, but He will not open the latch. This is our freedom of choice. He may not give us the foretaste of delight. The conversion might be likened to His "putting his hand to the door." He gives us a foretaste of what Divine Marriage with Him could mean but we alone can open our heart, our Soul, to His coming. Yes, we are so thrilled in the deepest part of our being. Our entire body is touched, but it is only a beginning. And if we don't let Him in completely, then we may lose our chance.

Many believe that conversion, or being "born again," is the end, but it is the beginning. Many misinterpret their cosmic experience as Marriage with God. This may be true in some cases. Each Soul is different in its experience. But there is much cleansing that follows conversion, usually. And the "Dark Night of the Soul," so called by St. John of the Cross, may have to be gone through. Our Bride is coming to that experience.

The myrrh was a precondition of the sorrow that would come upon the Bride. The sorrow of not having responded to the Bridegroom, letting nothing detain her.

In the parallel of the Kundalini going to meet the Shakti, or Universal Love, it may be blocked in the lower chakras by lack of faith, by fear of rejection, by negative thoughts, by sexual lust. Much is lost in sexual lust. Perhaps our Bride interpreted these feelings as physical desire for sex. That often drives away the opportunities for the soul to unite with God. The Kundalini when beginning its journey up the spine may be stopped at the sex organs and the feeling of passion. "I was thrilled that he was near" (Good News Bible) or "my heart began to pound for him" (New International Version) may stop our progress. Yes, of course, sexual desire is normal and can be a holy experience. But here we are talking about desire for the spiritual Bridegroom, and we may lose Him if we allow our sexual needs to eat up our emotions and our energy.

The myrrh may have been left by the Bridegroom as he realized the soul was blocked by sexual fantasies. Thus the Bride picked up sorrow, called for the Bridegroom, searched for Him. But it was too late. Too many blocks stood in the way.

And our agony, our true sorrow begins. The "Dark Night of the Soul" begins.

VERSE 6

I opened to my beloved,
    but my beloved had turned and gone.
My soul failed me when he spoke.
I sought him, but found him not;
    I called him, but he gave no answer.

Too late. We allow ourselves to be concerned with how we look, about our physical condition. We block our Soul from freely responding. And when we finally open to Him, He is gone. Often fear is the greatest block. "I called him, but he gave no answer." The Dark Night begins.

The Dark Night is a period that follows deep mystical searching. It may be like a period of exhaustion and may lead us to a time of rest from mystical matters in order to recuperate. Sometimes it comes on when we have made our greatest step forward. Sometimes it is physical illness or a psychological break into depression and disillusionment. It is a type of purification. Progress in contemplation may include light and shadow. God seems to be playing "hide and seek." This often happens previous to the birth of a new state of awareness.

We may experience great disharmony between ourselves and others in our life. We may be reminded of some cleansing that needs to be done in our consciousness so we can find our Lover, God. It feels at times as though we had lost Him completely. But if we can remember that our Soul, the Spark of that Divine, is waiting to guide us, we will survive.

Some seekers choose death of the physical body and chance a better life on the other side of death. Some may suicide. There is a fine line between the desire to live in order to have schooling on this plane and the desire to "chuck it all."

A woman I knew went through several years of the Dark Night. She was seeking God, but her marriage, her previous marriages, her arrested alcoholism, her physical disabilities were just too much. She was seeking the Mystical Marriage, but she finally gave up and succumbed to a new experience in another dimension.

Another friend went through years of separation from her grown children and suffered agony of spirit and of mind. But she held on, learned the lessons this experience brought, cleared her unconscious and conscious mind of her negative thoughts and actions which this experience brought to her awareness. Finally reconnected with her deep Inner Soul, she is on her way to the Mystical Marriage. The Dark Night can be surmounted by continuous faith in God.

It would appear at times that we have lost Him completely.

VERSE 7

The watchmen found me,
as they went about the city;

The wounded soul goes forth in search of God. It left the house of materialism where other people and attachments to physical existence were. It gave up all and went alone to search for the Lover. This is necessary, for if one does not find God, death will come. Remember, this experience comes after conversion, and after meditation and contemplation have been practiced. The Soul is awake and searching for Oneness. The Soul must leave behind that which hinders its progress. Our consciousness of God cannot be turned back.

Negative thoughts assail us in the Dark Night. The city is our place of consciousness. Our negative thoughts, the watchmen, attack the Soul and wound and weaken its desire for God, if we allow them. They are there, and somehow we must get away from them.

VERSE 7 (cont'd)

they beat me, they wounded me,
    they took away my mantle,
    those watchmen of the walls.

The mantle is called the veil in the King James Version.

The watchmen of the walls, that self-protection that we have built around our consciousness, are trying to dissuade us in our search. They take away our veil which on a physical level was the shame of that time, for a woman. But the veil hiding our searcher needs to be taken away. That is what stands between us and our full view of God. When this happens we may be stripped of self-will or the sensual attachment to the physical. The watchmen are often our greatest helpers, or the watchmen may be those qualities in our mind that keep us from Oneness. They are what beat us and wound us. But we can overcome them once the veil is removed from our full awareness of Reality and we become stronger.

VERSE 8

I adjure you, O daughters of Jerusalem,
    if you find my beloved,
that you tell him
    I am sick with love.

And then in this verse the Soul is speaking to our feminine side that produces the positive awareness of our Spirit. This side of our thinking is being changed. Positive awareness of our Spirit is happening. For often in the Dark Night we have lost touch with the feminine side of our psyche. This is true of both men and women. When we cease being so aggressive, active, rushing from here to

there to seek our Lover, God, and instead rest in meditation, love, creativity, compassion, gentleness, then we
shall come back to seeing our God and move on. When we
stop long enough to let the feminine speak to us and admit "I am sick with love" for His holiness, we begin to see
Him as He truly is.

Our Soul searches for Him. Our Soul is sick until it finds
Him. Our Soul is our feminine side. Our Soul sees Him in
all His radiant Being. We must come back to our soul and
let the physical, the psychological, the frantic searching go.
We must rest in contemplation and experience His Presence again as described in Verses 10–16. It is Love that our
Soul seeks.

VERSE 9

What is your beloved more than another beloved,
    O fairest among women?
What is your beloved more than another beloved,
    that you thus adjure us?

The old consciousness—the daughters of Jerusalem—has
placed its adoration, its love, on the outer, on other
beloveds.

So often in our human choices of a mate, of possessions,
of experiences we believe we have the best. Here, however,
the Soul is finding its true beloved, its true mate. It is God
the Beloved. And God never disappoints us. Our real soulmate is God. The Bride answers in the next verse. She
describes the perfect Cosmic Man.

VERSES 10–16

My beloved is all radiant and ruddy,
    distinguished among ten thousand.

His head is the finest gold;
  his locks are wavy,
  black as a raven.
His eyes are like doves
  beside springs of water,
bathed in milk,
  fitly set.
His cheeks are like beds of spices,
  yielding fragrance.
His lips are lilies,
  distilling liquid myrrh.
His arms are rounded gold,
  set with jewels.
His body is ivory work,
  encrusted with sapphires.
His legs are alabaster columns,
  set upon bases of gold.
His appearance is like Lebanon,
  choice as the cedars.
His speech is most sweet,
  and he is altogether desirable.
This is my beloved and this is
    my friend,
  O daughters of Jerusalem.

How poetic, how beautiful! How this passage raises us up from the mundane and puts us into an ecstatic frame of mind as we imagine all of this beauty as describing the Lover, our Higher Self!

Ruddy and white, King and Queen, sun and moon, brother-sister conjunctions mean the union with one's Self, Self-fertilization, Self-regeneration, Self-creation. All of this coming together of opposites appears in the Song of Songs. And we have some of this conjunction here.

These verses give us a vision of the pure love that our aspirant seeks. The Bride is speaking and describing the beauty, power, radiance, Divinity of the perfected Being. As always, we resort to the human qualities to express our highest experience of Divinity. Often while in a state of contemplation, one will have a realization that is beyond description. Here we are being introduced to a great being which symbolizes all that the meditator can imagine the Universal Being to be.

In the description we are given those material objects that describe the highest, the most beautiful, the strongest. Some of them are gold, doves, milk, lilies, ivory, jewels, sapphires, marble (alabaster), Lebanon cedars. This lifts our imagination and we may see our own perfect being that calls us on. And in Verse 16 she says, "This is my beloved, this is my friend." How wonderful to have such a friend!

In other places in the Bible we have the great Being described. In Daniel 10 and Revelation 10 we also have a description of such a Being. This is often called the Cosmic Man, and it appears in many religious descriptions. It is a symbol of the Self. This often comes to one in dreams or meditation and generally indicates a creative solution to a conflict. Only one is seen. The Persian Gayomart, the Hindu Purusha, the Chinese P'an Ku are the same as this Cosmic Man. It is of course an inner psychic image and is immortal. Many identify him with Christ, Buddha, Krishna, all great religious figures. When the ego merges with the Self, the vision occurs. Our Bride, our Soul, has experienced the Self in the Cosmic Man. I understand this because the vision I experienced had some of these qualities.

This Cosmic Man represents God and human as one. Indeed, the entire universe is One in this Being. The mineral kingdom: gold, jewels, marble; the vegetable kingdom: cedar, lilies, spices, myrrh; the animal kingdom: raven, dove; the human kingdom: physical body—are described; all are mentioned. The Cosmic Man contains all kingdoms or exemplifies all kingdoms. The Universal Energy is in all.

In Verse 11, gold is the purity we seek after the dross has been removed from our life. Gold represents the redeemed and regenerated Soul. Birds symbolize high spiritual activity.

In Verse 12, the dove is our symbol of peace.

In Verse 13, spices, as we have already noted, preserve for eternity. The lily is gold and white, colors which are always considered highly spiritual.

In Verse 14, jewels are filled with light, and they sparkle as bright as the sun. Jewels represent spiritual truths.

In Verse 15, the reference to Lebanon has to do with the spirit body. The cedars of Lebanon could not be destroyed by fire.

In Verse 16, the words that come from this vision are most sweet. He is altogether desirable. All in this vision gives us, in our own imagination, a Being that is most beautiful and the answer to our Search. Unconsciously we want to have this beautiful appearance.

This Being, this Self, this One, is where we are tending. The reason for our Journey is to become One with This, and the radiance attracts us to the Pure Light of which He is. He is altogether desirable, and the Soul is beloved. We are now ready, we are prepared for the Mystic Marriage. We are ready to experience the marriage of the Soul with the Cosmic Being. We are lifted up to the music of the spheres, the pure Light. For the body, mind, soul, and spirit are ready for the Cosmic Union. One must have the personal experience to understand the mystery clearly.

Chapter Six of
The Song of Songs

Now we come to the experience of the Mystic Marriage, Divine Marriage, Enlightenment in this Book of Love or Song of Love. For, of course, it is the expression of pure Love that elevates the Marriage above all marriages. It is Love that the Soul seeks and finds in our concept of the Universal Love that is available to all. Any feeling of ecstasy is a feeling of deep Love. Any need that we call by any other name is a need for Love. It is Love that we long for. Unfortunately, we may use up this life span in pursuit of Love and come to the end unfulfilled. It is Love that we seek.

It can take on many masks, this Love we search for. It may be masked as wisdom, knowledge, passion, intuition, power, joy, prosperity. But when these masks are removed we find Pure Love. We have named It God. We have no real understanding of It, or at least we cannot describe It. It can only be experienced or expressed. "Love is not love until you give it away."

The writer of the Song tried to explain Love. The various mystics, saints, and adepts have tried but always fall short of describing It. Our human vocabulary does not reach that high. It is too much for words. The Eastern mystic when asked to describe God replied, "Anyone who tries to describe or define God will have a face as red as the root of the beet." Such it is with Love. God is Love.

Because this great secret is so important to the evolution of humankind, the mystic tries through art, music, dance, thought, word, and deed to explain the goal of the pilgrim. It is useless, for each Soul has a different experience as it unites with Universal Love. But hoping to light a spark of desire in the breast of the beginner, the mystic describes the Path and the Goal. Thus we shall continue on.

The mystic practices an art. It has very little to do with the intellect. It is the creative in music, poetry, dance, art. It is raising this consciousness to the Absolute—establishing his conscious relationship with the Absolute. And then "I am God" is Truth.

The mystic leans toward poetry as a means of expressing the ineffable joy, passion, and love he/she feels. Poetry, as in the Song of Songs, lends itself to abstract expressions of deep Truth. It is cloaked, often in simile and metaphor, but the kernel of meaning is available to one who has had the mystical experience or is seeking it.

Thus the Song of Songs means something different to the mystic than it does to beginners on the Path.

VERSE 1

[The Chorus:]
Whither has your beloved gone,
    O fairest among women?
Whither has your beloved turned,
    that we may seek him with you?

She, the Bride, has not yet found her Beloved, even though she has had a vision of Him. But she knows where He is. The old consciousness, the chorus, in a sense is questioning the Soul's journey. It is imposing doubt as a block, for it implies, "If you know all this about Him, we want to go with you to find him." But the Soul knows, our Soul knows, where He can be found. He can be found in the garden, in our haven of beauty and potential growth. In the garden, our inner awareness, He is to be found.

VERSE 2

My beloved has gone down to his garden,
    to the beds of spices,
to pasture his flock in the gardens,
    and to gather lilies.

In John 15:1, 2 we have an interesting reference from the words of Jesus, (New International Version): "I am the true vine, my Father is the gardener. He cuts off every branch in me that bears no fruit, while every branch that does bear fruit he trims clean so that it will be even more fruitful." When we realize that Jesus is referring to the Christ that is within each of us, we can understand this better. For it is the Christ that is God, and it is that Christ which is our Soul. Later in Verse 4 he says, "Remain in me and I will remain in you. No branch can bear fruit by itself, it must remain in the vine. Neither can you bear fruit unless you remain in me [the Christ]."

There are those interpreters of this Song who see a third identity in the Song of Songs. The young shepherd is part of the description, they believe. Here it would seem strange to suggest that the Bride was referring to the Universal Energy as "pasturing his flock."

Because Jesus Christ was often referred to as the good shepherd, one might suggest that this passage referred to him. Jesus Christ and God are One.

God is the shepherd of all. It is He who leads us as sheep, who protects us from the wolves, who cares for us when we are ill or despondent. God is always in our garden. The Bride is here recognizing Him. Jesus Christ expressed God fully, and he is also with us in the form of his teachings, in his words, in his ideas, and in his spirit. He is the same as the Christ within. Jesus the Christ is the Good Shepherd, a manifestation of God.

VERSE 3

I am my beloved's and my beloved is mine;
    he pastures his flock among the lilies.

There are eight references to lily or lilies in this short Book. It is a very important symbol of wholeness, beauty, completion, purity, self growth. ("Consider the lilies of the field," Jesus said when he assured us that we did not need to worry about what we were to wear.) It symbolizes gold and white, wisdom, light-filled chakras, love. It is a well-chosen example of the perfection that is produced in the spiritual consciousness. It is interesting that the lily has become the flower that we think of at Easter. Easter is the celebration of the resurrection of Jesus and also the reminder of our own resurrection; and the resurrection is the same as becoming fully Enlightened and overcoming death.

Flocks are Souls that God sees or cares for in spiritual consciousness (the garden) that have not made the great step into Oneness. They are in a place of purity and He gathers them one by one.

VERSE 4

You are beautiful as Tirzah, my love,
    comely as Jerusalem,
        terrible as an army with banners.

The Bridegroom is now describing the Bride. Tirzah is a very delightful aspect of thought and of Soul. Jerusalem means peace, harmony, prosperity. In man the abiding consciousness of spiritual peace comes as a result of continuously keeping thoughts filled with love and peace. It is indeed a place of beauty. This is the New Jerusalem, which is symbolic of perfection.

An army with banners may indicate victory. Thus the victory over the opposition to Spiritual Marriage is being described. Peace, delight, and victory are at hand.

VERSE 5

Turn away your eyes from me,
>   for they disturb me—
Your hair is like a flock of goats,
>   moving down the slopes of Gilead.

The key is Gilead. Gilead symbolizes "mass of witnesses" and "enduring rock."

There are a mass of witnesses that this is the path to perfection which all of mankind makes in various ways. The ages have brought us many men and women who have achieved this high state of Godward awareness and who are surrounding us now and leading us on. The goats are animals that climb higher than most can go. We who are mystics on the mystic Path have also climbed the high mountain of Gilead, are aware of our Divinity, and are witnesses to others as we step into our responsibility of serving others, thus to lead them up Mt. Gilead to become still other witnesses.

(Verses 6 through 12 are from the New International Version of the Bible.)

VERSE 6

Your teeth are like a flock of sheep
    coming up from the washing.
Each has its twin,
    not one of them is alone.

Again the physical is used. The sheep are you and I. The
sheep are white and clean—all is forgiven, we are pure. We
have been washed in God's love. Our Soul has always been
spotless. It is our intellect and our emotions and our body
that needed washing and cleansing. The twins are the masculine and feminine in balance. We are being shown our
twin Soul.

VERSE 7

Your temples behind your veil
    are like the halves of a pomegranate.

The veil is still over the face of the Beloved. She is still
not quite complete. But the potential for great fecundity
is there—the pomegranate is full of seeds. Also the
pomegranate is both red and white. This may designate the
physical—red blood—and the spiritual, white. Oneness is
there but still not fully open to God's glory.

VERSES 8, 9

Sixty queens there may be,
    and eighty concubines,
    and virgins beyond number;
but my dove, my perfect one, is unique,
    the only daughter of her mother,
    the favorite of the one who bore her.
The maidens saw her and called her blessed;
    the queens and concubines praised her.

These two verses deal with the feminine. Queens, concubines, virgins, maidens—women that are related to sexual activity with men on the physical level. But we are discussing the Song from a spiritual level. What do these verses teach us?

The queen implies a king. The concubines imply beautiful women. The virgin is one who is pure. The maiden is a young woman without blemish.

Each of us has all of these as a part of his/her spiritual potential. The queen of heaven is married to the masculine concept of God which has come down through the ages. This was the Jewish concept of God—masculine. So, naturally, the Soul is feminine as it approaches marriage to the Universal Energy we call God. Waiting in the wings are the concubines. Those are the Souls that aspire to the high calling of the mystic but cannot or will not take the step. They seem to have no self-motivation or self-control. But they are nearer to the king than most.

The virgins are those Souls that have not yet tasted the glory of a close relationship with God. They are pure in the sense that they have not been touched yet by the world. But they will be touched by the King, for they are in His court.

The lover says, "But my dove, my perfect one is unique." The Soul, the dove, the perfect one has reached the point of completion. This one is becoming One, is One, with God. This one has been wooed by God, has responded, and is being married to God. This Divine Marriage is so far above the earth marriage that she, the Soul, is said to be the favorite of the one who bore her.

Now who bore the Soul? On the spiritual level it is Father/Mother God that gives birth to the Soul, to the Beloved. It is to Him/Her to whom each Soul is returning as it is recognized by the conscious mind as being purity balanced in the masculine/feminine aspect. Other maidens, queens, concubines bless her at the Wedding and praise her, for they know of her purity in Marriage. They are near enough to the throne to realize unity.

VERSE 10

Who is this that appears like the dawn,
    fair as the moon, bright as the sun,
    majestic as the stars in procession?

Dawn, light, planets, sun, moon, stars. The high and holy place of the planets is not accepted by humankind to day as it continues to rely on the scientific process to "prove" all truth. In the days of the writing of the Song the planets and stars served as objects of worship, as predictors of the future, as explanation of the present. Astrology was the forerunner of astronomy, and although the scientific astronomers say they do not believe in astrology, they, like the young astronomer researcher I met in Russia, find it an intriguing concept which is not quite scientific but has many truths in it.

High above the earth they pass night and day, day and night. The sun lights our way by day, the moon reflects the light to earth by night, the stars are their own light. All of this is used to say to the Beloved, ''You are the sun. You too reflect the Light, you too are your own Light. It is Light you are. You are the dawn. You are fair as the moon, bright as the sun, majestic as the stars as you go on your course completely in rhythm with the balance of the Universe. You are That, you are One with the Sun, Moon, Stars. You are the Universe. You are Light and only Light. You are One with All!''

Sometimes this high experience comes to us even though we may not have consciously been on a spiritual journey. It may come as a great surprise either during or after an experience that has shaken us out of our routine. It may be a happy experience that brings it about, but more often it is a devastating experience that has knocked down all our defenses.

Gopi Krishna, an Enlightened Hindu, says that a near-death experience may bring it about. Also when one is willing to give up all in her/his world and with confidence and joy is ready to leave it, the Mystic Marriage is performed. It is a giving of all to God, to be One with God. I believe my Divine Marriage occurred at just such a time after I had been on a conscious spiritual journey for many years.

I was ill with vomiting and diarrhea. After the third day I became faint. The medics rushed me by helicopter to the nearest hospital. They thought I was dying.

In the emergency room the nurses and attendants were rushing around taking care of me. I realized they thought I was dying. I was fully conscious and asked my Inner Self why I felt so alive. The answer was, "Because you will always be alive. There is no death. There is only life." I replied, "In that case, I am ready to let go of this body and go on with life elsewhere." The answer was, "No you have other tasks to perform before you do that." I then saw a vision of a river of light flowing in both directions. There was no fear. I was freed of all fear of death. I had willingly given up all relationships and possessions. I chose to leave but I was healed.

Later I learned that I had a bleeding ulcer, had lost over half of my blood. I never had any pain before or after. I am convinced I had this experience to remove all fear of death and to realize I was free of the world.

It was several days before I was well enough to know this Truth. During those days I went through various stages of what I call resurrection.

I lost touch with my Inner Self. I could not touch my God with my thought or in the Silence. Then I seemed to be in a hole surrounded by dirt, roots, and stubble. Then I was among thousands of people and their attention focused upon me. Then I was shown pictures of little storybook animals cavorting and playing. It was like a child's book filled with colorful pictures of a pony, a bear, a dog. All were entertaining me, and I laughed with joy. (I have since been reminded of Jesus' teaching found in Matthew 18:3—"Truly, I say to you, unless you turn and become like children, you will never enter the kingdom of Heaven.") And then I was back in touch with my Inner Self. All was well. Later I crocheted and embroidered nursery-like scenes, which grounded this experience.

My life turned around after that. Oh, I don't mean my evolution was complete. Oh, no. I had a challenge with relationships. I made mistakes in investment. But I was completely free of fear and I loved God with such depth that I could not describe it. Ecstasy of love welled up in me all the time, and my life became happier and happier. I have written three books since then and continue to teach others in classes and seminars.

This high state, this Enlightenment that mystics seek and find, is complete. The Soul has come full circle and takes its place with Universal Harmony. We are all aware of our Oneness with All and so in a sense are always Enlightened. Still, our conscious mind must be convinced. Being "Home" is beyond description.

VERSES 11, 12

I went down to the grove of nut trees
    to look at the new growth in the valley,
to see if the vines had budded
    or the pomegranates were in bloom.

Before I realized it,
    my desire set me among the royal
      chariots of my people.
[*King James Version: the chariots of Amminadib*]

The Soul, the Beloved, speaks. The Soul has found its home among the stars, with the sun and moon. The Soul has reached the High Estate. But it is pulled back to the earth, for it must serve humankind after it reaches this Oneness. Emma Curtis Hopkins calls God the Great Servitor. He serves us, His Universal Mind moves us, He takes care of us. When we are One with Him through the Mystic Marriage, then we take on this responsibility. We too must serve; as mystics, we must serve as God serves.

The Beloved goes to a grove of nut trees. Nuts are symbols of Truth surrounded by a hard shell that needs to be broken so that we can partake of the Truth within. The new growth in the valley (physical living) is the new thinking, the new truth (which is old) that human beings are learning, accepting, and thus producing. The vines have budded, the fruit of the Spirit will follow and will feed humankind.

Amminadib means generous and broadminded in spiritual thinking. The desire of the Soul is to be among those Aspirants who are generous and broadminded in spiritual thoughts and are ready to be taught, to be served, to be awakened.

It may be that the Soul, when Enlightened, will choose to leave its present physical body and reincarnate in another body to serve mankind at a higher level. This may be the genius in science, music, arts, literature, physical culture, religion, philosophy, psychology. It will serve in an area that will lift human beings to a higher level. If it should lose the realization of its Oneness while living in the physical world, the physical life may end in tragedy. If it remembers from whence the genius comes, from where these advanced thoughts spring, it will serve out its time in dignity and beauty. The aim of the Universe is to bring all humanity to Oneness, and that is the responsibility of the genius. These special Souls may serve in very servile roles. They are usually humble and quiet. But their influence is felt none the less, and the broadminded and the generous are drawn into their circle of influence, and thus the Soul is "set among the royal chariots of my people."

Or the Soul after this Mystic Marriage may remain on earth in its present body and bring Truth to humankind through many avenues.

This awareness of Oneness can happen at any age, but we wonder, when men and women do their greatest work after the age of 60 and sometimes into their 80s, whether the Mystic Marriage has happened to them late in life. Sometimes it is not until one is released from the duty of making a living and caring for a family that time and energy are released to devote to the Search. And then the miracle happens!

However, the spiritual dimension of awareness can come forth at any age, and genius follows. One of the best arguments for reincarnation is our observation of the very young, four or five years old, who seem to have advanced knowledge that puts them in a genius class. I believe they have an old Soul that has had the Mystic Marriage in a former life and that they have come back to serve humanity.

(The remaining verses in this chapter are taken from the R.S.V. Bible unless noted.)

VERSE 13

Return, return, O Shulammite,
    return, return, that we may look
        upon you.

This was spoken by the chorus or the friends. This is the collective unconscious that affects all of us on our journey for it is based on past and present actions and thoughts of the human race. It is history as well as present. We all adore history even though it contains all the pains and ills and mistakes of the human race as well as its beauty and evolution. But we tend to be afraid of future change and think we can base our present choices on the past. Of course, the past is a part of the present and the present affects us also. But we must be guided by the Inner Guide, not by what is conventional. We should let go of the advice of the multitude.

Shulammite means peace and perfection. Our Bride, our Soul, is at this high point without problems, without desires, without pain, without the negatives of the human condition. But the collective unconscious, human thought, tries to call her back. It appeals to the ego. It wants to gaze on her—an appeal to the ego. But perfection and peace do not need to come back, for the Soul is at One. The ego has been transformed.

VERSE 13 (cont'd)

Why should you look upon the Shulammite,
    as upon a dance before two armies?

The Soul answers: "You do not need to gaze at perfection and peace for it is One with God. I shall not be disturbed by the collective unconscious. It must cleanse itself."

Two armies together means that the duality has become unity. Our Soul is no longer separate but has gone home to the Godhead. No more conflict. All is peace, and the celebration of the dance is enjoyed.

The Shulammite has been called the Divine Sophia, the Philosopher's Stone of the alchemist, the Beloved Lady of the Epistle of John. The feminine has become One with the masculine, which is inherent in these other names.

Shulammite is said by some scholars to represent the feminine side of Solomon. Again, this fits the idea of the Soul's being feminine and at One with the Godhead.

We are not through. There are other representations of this awesome experience as we go on.

Chapter Seven of
The Song of Songs

Chapter 7 gives us a description of what we shall be in the physical, emotional, mental, and spiritual aspects when we are Married. It is a beautiful chapter that lifts us to new heights.

Beauty and love form the central core of the definition of God by the mystic. Throughout this Song we have been brought to the visualization of great beauty of all that is on our planet—trees, flowers, gardens, animals, the sky, the human body in its Light state, the beauty of Love itself. This beauty gives us harmony, balance, and design. And this love and beauty form a correlation in our mind, in our imagination, of what the glory of God is when we are at One with Him. And in the Silence, through meditation, it is the most ecstatic Beauty.

Verses 1-5 of this chapter are describing the maid (Soul) and the body, which has become pure Spirit, pure Light. The passage describes the physical transformed into pure Spirit. The body is never as beautiful in the physical as in the Light. The Soul shines through the physical and illumines each cell, and we are no longer physical. We are Beauty!

It is necessary now to explain in more detail the changing of the physical body into pure Light, for these five verses are describing the result of being at One.

An ancient Eastern teaching (see Ch. 1) says that an energy lies dormant at the base of our spine which it calls the Kundalini. Through various physical and spiritual practices it can be awakened, and it courses up the spine to meet the pineal and pituitary glands in the head. When these two conjoin, they cause the experience of Bliss, and Enlightenment occurs. As the Kundalini goes up the spine, it opens certain energy plexus in the etheric body. These are called chakras. These chakras are attached to the physical body at the endocrine centers. As they are opened, they affect the physical body. It vibrates at a higher rate and eventually is transformed into vibrating energy. This body, transformed, can be seen by the physical eyes of those who have been prepared. (John, Peter, and James saw Jesus transformed on the Mount of Transfiguration—Matthew 17:2.)

When we are One in consciousness, we may assume this form as Jesus did. At his Ascension he became this Light body.

This description of the transformed body (Verses 1–5) denotes the highest level of consciousness of Divinity that humankind is capable of experiencing. (Read *Kundalini: The Evolutionary Energy in Man*, by Gopi Krishna, for further details.)

VERSE 1

How graceful are your feet in sandals,
O queenly maiden!

The entire body is aflame with the Light. The feet being on the earth also have energy from the Earth. The queen is being addressed.

VERSE 1 (cont'd)

Your rounded thighs are like jewels,
   the work of a master hand.

The thighs are connected to the body at the location of
the "home" of the Kundalini. This chakra center when
vibrating at a high rate gives off sparks of light as a jewel.
It is the work of a master hand, for Kundalini is that spark
of God that impregnates our physical as well as our mental and emotional being.

VERSE 2

Your navel is a rounded bowl
   that never lacks mixed wine.

The navel is in the area of the sex organs and is the location of the second chakra. The sex organs are full of the
energy of procreation. They transform the fruit of the body
into the fluids necessary for their activity. This fruit is like
wine. Here it is that we may find our greatest challenge to
achieving Oneness.

VERSE 2 (cont'd)

Your belly is a heap of wheat,
   encircled with lilies.

Wheat symbolizes the seed of spirit growing into mortal thought. Lilies, as we have noted, are symbols of purity.
   The belly is in the vicinity of the solar plexus, a great
power center in the body. Some say the mind is located
here, with the brain acting as a computer. When this
center is open our thoughts are pure, and they make all
mortal thoughts pure. It indicates the transformation of the
physical needs to the needs of pure spirit.

VERSE 3

> Your two breasts are like two fawns,
> twins of a gazelle.

At the breast location is the fourth chakra, often called the heart chakra. The heart chakra has always been connected with love, and so the love center is open and is seen as twin fawns of a gazelle.

The gazelle symbolizes swift, graceful movement. The two breasts symbolize balance. So the love chakra, when open, allows us to be swiftly and gracefully loving with perfect balance.

Oh how wonderful when we reach that point in our spiritual development! We love continuously, we know when to let go if our love is rejected, we keep in balance the love of our self and love of others, we reach the apex of loving as Jesus taught: "You shall love the Lord thy God with all your heart and with all your soul and with all your mind. . . . You shall love your neighbor as yourself" (Matthew 22:36, 39). This is our path. To love God first is where we have come from and is the goal we reach when we are Enlightened. Then the balance between love of self and neighbor is a given.

VERSE 4

> Your neck is like an ivory tower.

In the throat lies the fifth chakra. The throat is a place of power, for from it issue our words of praise or condemnation. But this neck is like an ivory tower. Ivory was a very precious substance used to build and decorate expensive buildings. The tower was a high place from which the surrounding country could be observed.

The use of the fifth chakra, the throat, brings some of

us the most precious of experiences. It is the source of so
much of our perfection as we use sound to lift the vibra-
tions of the body, mind, and emotions to a higher level. It
is within the tower of perfection, and it makes us more
perfect as we use it for the Word of God. The fifth chakra
gives us a dignity and power that are lacking when it is
closed.

VERSE 4 (cont'd)

Your eyes are pools in Heshbon,
    by the gate of Bath-rabbim.
Your nose is like a tower of Lebanon,
    overlooking Damascus.

Heshbon symbolizes understanding, intelligence, inven-
tion, intuition. Bath-rabbim means measure of greatness.
Between the eyes is the sixth chakra, designated as the
Third Eye, which many see as wisdom. It is apparent when
intelligence and love are brought together, the thought and
feeling—when the Soul and the Christ are One. Then we
have intuition. This is basic to all inventions, all creativity, and to a good life. So these lines are reiterating what
we know. This chakra opened gives us intuition, which is
wisdom from God.

The eyes are truly the windows of the Soul. When one
is privileged to experience a vision, the eyes may be the
most prominent part of the vision.

These eyes, fully opened to Truth, are pure and look out
upon Damascus (body sensation) with wisdom. "The eye
is the lamp of the body. So if your eye is sound your whole
body will be full of light, but if your eye is not sound, your
whole body will be full of darkness" (Matthew 6:22, 23).
Jesus was speaking.

Lebanon has been explained in Chapter 3:9. It means peace, brilliant, clean.

It is the opening of the Third Eye above the nose that is our intuitive quality, and when Jesus was speaking of the eye, not the eyes, he was speaking of this sixth chakra. Near this point lie the pituitary and pineal glands, which are so closely related to the experience of Enlightenment.

Verse 5

Your head crowns you like Mt. Carmel [*New
International Version*]
and your flowing locks are like purple;
a king is held captive in the tresses.

The head crowned like Mount Carmel is the location of the seventh chakra, often called the thousand-petaled lotus, for when open, it is like a flower with myriad streams of rays of light coming from it. Charles Fillmore says in the *Metaphysical Bible Dictionary*, "Mount Carmel stands for the center of spirituality, which is located in the body's consciousness at the top of the head" (p. 140, under "Carmel"). Jesus called this *Paradise* or freedom from sense.

Our maiden, our feminine, our Soul, has been Enlightened, and all are shining like the purple of royalty. For when Enlightened, we are royal, we are One with God, the King of All. Our body shows forth the radiance.

Verses 6, 7

How fair and pleasant you are,
O loved one, delectable maiden!
You are stately as a palm tree,
and your breasts are like
its clusters [*of fruit*].

How beautiful we are when we are married to our Lord! The maiden is never more beautiful than on her wedding day. She is surrounded by love, she breathes love, she shines with love. Oh how wonderful if we could always show forth this love!

Carrying our comparison further, we see the palm tree bereft of branches, with the palm branches at the top—the seventh chakra gleaming with light shooting from the center of the crown. The clusters of fruit are a fitting simile for the breasts, which symbolize love and which give food for the newborn child. The milk of love and compassion flows from the breasts to the babe. And we are in that stage after we have experienced the Mystical Marriage. We exude love and the fullness of His Glory.

Verse 8

I say I will climb the palm tree
and lay hold of its branches.

The Beloved is so bright and shining that the Lover wants to be in that Light also. God is personified here as Solomon or the Lover. It is hard for us to place these words on His lips. But God is searching for our Soul. God is not complete until we return to Oneness with Him/Her. And the Lover rejoices in our beauty, our fruitfulness.

Verses 8 (cont'd), 9

Oh, may your breasts be like clusters of the vine,
and the scent of your breath like apples,
and your kisses like the best wine
that goes down smoothly,
gliding over lips and teeth.

Here we have "clusters of the vine," "apples," "wine." Again, we are moved to physical terms to explain our beauty after we experience the Marriage.

How much solace wine has brought to mankind! How much it has smoothed the way to live on this plane of seeming pain, duality, ups and downs! How it has been used for the celebration of our special events! It has made our life smoother. But of course, like all things of the earth, it is dual—and how it has brought sorrow, pain, and degradation! But here it is used in a positive sense. The Bliss that is being experienced is compared to the smoothness of the best wine and the pleasure it brings.

So, returning to our scripture, the fruitfulness expressed here is indicative of the results of the Divine Marriage. The fruits will continue to be produced.

Now the Soul speaks to the Beloved:

VERSE 10

I am my beloved's,
  and his desire is for me.

Oneness is here expressed. The Soul and God are One, and the feminine and masculine are together forever. "I am His and He is mine." How many love songs have been written around that theme without realizing the deeper meaning! Many love songs popular today can be interpreted in the light of the Soul's love for God and vice-versa. And love between a man and a woman is usually only a facsimile of this Love but can be the essence of it.

VERSES 11, 12

Come, my beloved,
  let us go forth into the fields,
  and lodge in the villages;

> let us go out early to the vineyards,
>   and see whether the vines have budded,
> whether the grape blossoms have opened
>   and the pomegranates are in bloom.
> There I will give you my love.

It is in the earth experience that we express our love for God. It is in the everyday living that we show forth our fruits. It is not in a cave in the Himalayas separated from all of mankind. It is in our daily life among the fields and villages.

In the East some Adepts, who have experienced the Mystic Marriage, often pull away from society and spend their life in meditation and prayer for the human race. In the West, our Adepts have been very involved in caring for the human beings they are guided to, in teaching, in writing, in expressing in the marketplace and in the temples, monasteries, and cathedrals. The saints of the Catholic church continued to carry out their duties after they were married to God. So the Soul and God as One go to the fields to bless them, to the villages to be among the people, for it was there that a living was earned. Nowadays the Adept is working in the middle of society—in government, education, religion, business to bring the blessing from God to the people of the earth. The Adept, however, finds much time to be alone with God.

The Adept eventually separates from those who are not interested in walking the Path. Sometimes the mystic has to leave behind relationships, possessions, vocations and find a new and different environment. The mystic is not usually full-blown perfect after the Mystic Marriage. The mystic still has challenges but having once had the experience of the Marriage is forever changed and may no longer fit into the old environment. All is changed. Perhaps

he/she will be given a new vocation to raise the consciousness of the world through teaching, preaching, writing, in
the theater, on television, in the movies. The Mystic Marriage can occur several times, but each time we reach a
higher dimension.

You may be asking, "How do I identify a mystic?" A
good question, for many who claim to be at One with God
are not. I would say, "By their fruits you shall know
them." The mystic is not bound up in his/her own will
but seeks always God's will, the Higher Self, to direct their
life. The mystic does not depend on a book, an institution,
a holy man, or a spirit guide for guidance. The Adept goes
within, and so turning within brings this guidance.

Enlightenment is inside, beyond politics, judgment,
security, certainty of the outer explanation. It just *is now*.
Expressing in the outer the Infinite that is within: this is
the major task of the mystic.

Most mystics do not advertise their profession. It is said
that "Those who know do not speak; those who speak do
not know." Many who have been converted, who have
practiced meditation and contemplation for years, are
Adepts but do not recognize it. If you are uncertain, you
might like to read some books that describe them. *Mysticism*, by Evelyn Underhill, is a classic.

There I will give you my love. (Verse 12)

The Bride, or the Lover, is saying to the other one, "It
is in service to others that I give you my love." How else
can we give our love to God and He to us if not to and
through other Souls in our world? The consummation of
the Marriage takes place among the people we choose to
be with. It is through service that the Bodhisattva expresses the true relationship with God. It was Jesus' service

to all of humankind on planet Earth that revealed God's
love for us. Only through our letting His Love flow through
us can we really be at One with Him. And we must be at
One with Him to let that Love flow freely. A paradox.

What does this mean, "I will give you my love"? To
whom are we giving our love? Is it not to our Self? Not just
love, but Love? For in loving our Self, we are at One with
God. That Self is the manifestation of God. Our Self is our
Soul, and we consciously love it.

VERSE 13

The mandrakes give forth fragrance,
 and over our doors are all choice fruits,
new as well as old,
 which I have laid up for you, O my beloved.

The Lover is speaking. All the good of the Universe
comes forth to us after we have accepted God as our
spouse, our love, our guide. It is all ours then, for we recognize that "I am That I AM." I AM is total Being. I AM is
the name of Love. We are that I AM, for we have returned
to our Father, we have left our prodigal ways and returned
Home. And the fragrance of all Life is ours. We have all
choice fruits of the Spirit, as Paul named them in Galatians
5:22—love, joy, peace, patience, kindness, goodness, faith-
fulness, gentleness, self-control. We have lost our desire
for anything that is not of the Spirit. All else fades, is a
passing parade, a dance of shadows, for desire is for our
One-and-Only Beloved, God the Good Omnipotent. We
are One, but we live as a being of Light and serve Him
through serving others.

God and the Soul have laid up a store of Good for each—
God and the Soul entwined, and no one, no thing, can

separate them. It is for Eternity. This is the true Marriage for Eternity. All is eternal.

I should like to quote several passages from the classic *Interior Castle*, written in the 1570s by St. Teresa of Avila, a Spanish Carmelite nun.

> The soul (I mean the spirit of the soul) is made one with God who, being likewise a spirit, has been pleased to reveal the love that He has for us by showing to certain persons the extent of that love, so that we may praise His greatness. For He has been pleased to unite Himself with His creature in such a way that they have become like two that cannot become separated from one another: even so He will not separate Himself from her.

> This [love], sisters, you will have experienced, for I think that when the soul reaches the Prayer of Union, the Lord begins to exercise this care over us if we do not neglect the keeping of His commandments. When this experience comes to you remember it belongs to the innermost Mansion (soul), where God dwells in our souls, and give Him fervent praise, for it is He who sends it to you, like a message or a letter, written very lovingly and in such a way that He would have you alone be able to understand what He has written and what He is asking of you in it.

And one more:

> These effects God bestows, together with all those other good effects already described in the above-mentioned degrees of prayer, when the soul approaches Him, and He also gives the soul that kiss for which the Bride besought Him; for I understand it to be in this Mansion [soul] that that petition is fulfilled.*

*St. Teresa of Avila, *Interior Castle*. E. Allison Peers, ed. and trans. (Garden City, N.Y.: Image Books, 1961), pp. 214, 222, 224.

Chapter Eight of
The Song of Songs

Our Song reached such a high point at the end of Chapter Seven that there seems no need to go further. Some scholars even believe that the chapters are out of order. However, we shall see in this chapter that there is more teaching for us as the Mystic Marriage is consummated. In Chapter Eight we have a recapitulation of Chapters One through Seven. The whole process is reviewed, sometimes in different terms. Repetition of the Enlightenment experience is not unusual.

The Soul speaks:

VERSE 1

O that you were like a brother to me,
    that nursed at my mother's breast!
If I met you outside, I would kiss you,
    and none would despise me.

This passage has confused many interpreters through the ages and indeed it could have many interpretations. It seems to me, though, that it is referring to our frustration with the abstract perception of God. The inability of the human mind to understand the numinosity, spiritual essence, of That which the Soul loves becomes very confusing. And so we again resort to familiar relationships, to statues, to amulets, etc., to express our feeling, our understanding.

A brother and sister were husband and wife in Egypt to protect the royal line from being fouled by common blood. In much of mythology a brother and sister marry as the god and goddess. And so the choice of a brother seems to relate to that. If God is our Father/Mother then the brother and sister have the same parentage and would be closer than if only one of the two had God for a parent.

Our longing is often portrayed in our choice of a spouse. We try to find a perfect being in the one we choose to marry. How disappointed we may be! It is really the spouse in the Divine Marriage we search for. Until we find *this* soulmate, we shall probably not find our soulmate in the physical.

Despite the ancient belief that God is masculine, we realize that Mary, a female, gave birth to the Jesus that became Jesus the Christ. He is our brother, for the spiritual self is born of the feminine. And we search out ways to bring the masculine in balance with the feminine. Here we have our brother nursing at our mother's breast. We are all born of the Spirit, and all are our brothers. Even the Lover in this Canticle is given birth by our feminine nature, for God is Love, and Love is considered feminine.

Could we see Jesus Christ as occupying the place of "a brother"? He came in human form, and we have been able to identify God through Jesus. He demonstrated God incarnate, he was kissed by the multitudes, and he nursed at the breast of Love. Our brother did come, and the Shulammite called for him.

It is frustrating, we think, not to express our love in a physical way, but it is so much more satisfying to express it through our Soul.

VERSE 2

I would lead you and bring you
    into the house of my mother,
    and into the chamber of her that
      conceived me.

We must remember that Jehovah, or God, is never named in this Book. We have assumed that Solomon is the King of earth and heaven and thus of the consciousness that each Soul is. We should also remember that God was feminine up to the time of the Aryan invasion of parts of the Near and Middle East. Then the Hebrews were influenced by this invasion and God became masculine.

The book *When God Was a Woman*, by Merlin Stone, a woman, traces the change from a female God to a male God. She suggests that the Hebrews after entering Canaan, for political reasons and inheritance rights, put down the female God of Astarte and insisted that God was male. Her books relating the archeological and historical findings give woman, the feminine, the Creatress role in the history of humankind. Christianity and Islam have followed the masculine God concept as their teachings are based on the Old and New Testaments. All of this has affected the status of women down to the present day.

In this verse the Soul is saying, "My mother conceived me." Is this an allusion to God as female? Is the Soul not only a spark of the Father but also fruit of the Mother God? The Soul is considered the Bride in this interpretation. The Soul is feminine and combining with God, the masculine aspect. This is, of course, based on the Old Testament teaching of God as male.

It doesn't really matter, as I see it. I view God as neither male nor female. We human beings have felt it necessary to make God one or the other. It depends, it would seem, on which sex has power over the other.

Another interpretation could, of course, be that the feminine element of the Godhead is the mother of the Soul, and Soul, the Bride, is now married to the Bridegroom, the Godhead, the masculine.

VERSE 3

O that his left hand were under my head,
    and that his right hand embraced me!

(See 2:6 also.)

The left hand of God and the right hand of God in the Bible seem to carry different messages.

Carl Jung thought that two hands joined signified the Mystical Marriage, or individuation, as he called it. The hands are seen as symbols of power. The right hand, masculine, may denote the rational, conscious, logical, while the left hand, feminine, denotes intuition, feelings, creativity. Here it would appear that the two hands of the Lover embracing the Soul denote balance of logic and intuition, which is the case when one has experienced the Mystic Marriage. All is in balance.

Verse 4 is very similar to Chapter 2:7.

VERSE 4

I adjure you, O daughters of Jerusalem,
    that you stir not up nor awaken love
    until it please.

Here the daughters of Jerusalem, the old way of thinking, are again warned that love must not be awakened until there is no alternative. To awaken Divine Love within our consciousness will change our entire life. Many of our old habits, possessions, understandings, relationships will have to be dropped, and not without pain. But the ecstasy described in this Book is well worth the pain caused by stirring up and awakening Love.

VERSE 5

Who is that coming up from the wilderness,
        leaning upon her beloved?

The answer to the question is in the next two lines. It is the Bride, the Soul, coming from the wilderness (earth consciousness, the experience on earth without God's guidance). This ascent is a difficult undertaking when we try it alone. These difficulties, of course, teach us—but when we reach out to God and allow Him/Her to support us, then the way is cleared for the ascension. We are surrounded by the wilderness of the collective unconscious and race consciousness. We are drawn back from the ascent time after time by our attachment to things of the world. But leaning on our Inner Guide, the Bridegroom, gives us the strength and the knowing that we will reach Home.

VERSE 5 (cont'd)

Under the apple tree I awakened you.
There your mother was in travail with you,
        there she who bore you was in travail.

According to Corinne Heline (*New Age Bible Interpretation*, vol. 1), the word *apple* derives from an old Egyptian word meaning evil. In Latin also the word *malum* means apple and evil. This apple or evil is open to change and can be made pure and holy. Many of the great avatars in mankind's mythology and history have been born under a tree.

The Lover is saying that under the shade of evil the Bride was awakened and began her Life. When we speak of this, we are saying that the consciousness of our Divinity was awakened. How often we are in the dregs of physical living when we are awakened to our potential!

The mother is our feminine aspect, or love, that gives birth to this awareness. How much travail it goes through before we admit our need to have a "new birth," a "rebirth"—to be born again—! But God, our Lover, knows—and is forever urging us, nudging us to be reborn under the Tree of Life, of Eternal Life. We are taken from the apple-tree consciousness.

VERSE 6

Set me as a seal upon your heart,
    as a seal upon your arm;

The Lover continues to speak. This seal set on the heart and on the arm is like the ring exchanged in a physical marriage. It says, "This person is married to God." The Soul is married to God, and the Soul now expresses freely in love (heart) and in service (arm). The Soul is completely pledged to God.

This, of course, is what the mystic sees as the goal. It may have been searched for in many lifetimes. To pledge our love and our service to God is our devotion, and the seal is apparent as others observe our life. The seal I would see as the Christ, which is expressing through the soul. We are sealed with the Christ. Paul writes in 2 Corinthians 1:21, 22, "Now it is God who makes both us and you stand firm in Christ. He anointed us, set his seal of ownership on us, and put his Spirit in our hearts as a deposit, guaranteeing what is to come" (New International Version). Thus we have all the blessings and power of God, for we are One with Him. We are En-light.

VERSE 6 (cont'd)

for love is strong as death,
    jealousy (passion) is cruel as the grave.
Its flashes are flashes of fire,
    a most vehement flame.

Do you see how strong this seal of Love is? It overcomes death, for there is no death ever again, as the Soul is One. Death was made a very fearful experience in the Old Testament. Jesus taught that death was not to be feared, for there is no death but only eternal life. And it is Love that wipes away all fear of death, for when our Soul is One, we need not stay on or return to this planet of death. Love overcomes the fear of death.

When the body, mind, and emotions are transformed into pure Light, there is no death of the physical, for it is no more.

The word *jealousy* is translated as a passion in some Bibles. Passion is defined as desire, and desire can cause us to seek the grave. It can be evil if it is negative, as in the case of desire for sexual activity without love, which is lust. Lust has no place in Love, for Love does not possess, it liberates. Passion is a vehement flame. We are tried by our desires time after time. We rise above this when we truly Love. For Love is God, and we are Sons of God or are as God, and only Love can be expressed in our life when we have the Mystic Marriage experience.

Desire (passion) covers many other emotions besides lust. Desire or passion for anything can be "cruel as the grave'' when measured against love of God and only God. Desire for earth pleasure, for people, for things can divert us from life with the Spirit. The Eastern religions teach that we must become desireless in order to find God in the ultimate sense.

The dross in our consciousness is burned out by the *Fire* of passion. We learn that Love is the only answer. As our desires or passions lead us into troubles or cruelties we learn our lessons. Desire must be lost in spiritual thinking which is often symbolized by the element *Air*.

VERSE /

Many waters cannot quench love,
  neither can floods drown it.
If a man offered for love
  all the wealth of his house,
  it would be utterly scorned.

When the seal of God is upon our heart, nothing can change it, nothing can be given for it. For the seal of God is Love and is ours forever.

To speak of love without speaking of God is useless. Love comes from God, it is God. So often we mistake the feeling of passion for Love. And how many mistakes have occurred in your life, as well as in the lives of many others!

Love never is lost. Once we love another with God's Love, there is no emotion that can change it. *Water* is symbolic of emotion. No emotion, negative or positive, can change our love for another or for God.

Neither can it be bought. It is free. The greatest experience of a human being is to have this great feeling of Love for self, God, and another. How often we have tried to buy love with gifts, with possessions which are of *Earth* consciousness. How often we have tried to force it. All wealth cannot buy Love. It is freely received and freely given.

Our love is challenged by many of the human characteristics such as intellect, emotions, love of possessions, and passion. These can be related to the four elements—air, water, earth, and fire respectively—which the esotericist claims are blocks in our way as we ascend to a higher level of consciousness. All four are referred to in these verses. They are challenges that must be overcome and laid to rest if we are to reach Oneness.

These verses are a short summary of what we have come through to reach this high attainment of Divinity. Pure Love comes from our Love of God and following His Will. Love is stronger than any of the elements of our Being.

Verses 6 and 7 are a great canticle to Love. Indeed, the entire Book is a great hymn of praise to Love. How easily mankind has misinterpreted this Book as physical sex between a maid and a shepherd boy! It is an example of our inability to understand Love. Like God, Love is inexplicable and can only be understood as we rise in consciousness to our Divinity. Verses 6 and 7 say that if we put the seal of God on our heart, it will overcome all those human experiences that seem to prevent our climb to perfection.

Love is as strong as death, indeed it is as inevitable as death. For each of us has a Soul that is pure Love, that is pure Spirit, and it will be recognized and expressed in this life or another. It is inevitable. For this we are made and from this we are made.

Love flashes continuously as a flame. A flame of fire can cleanse, can make a metal pure, or it can destroy if used wrongly. Its sparks are seen by all as we allow it to shine forth.

Nothing can quench this fire of love, not even water (emotions). It burns forever and never goes out. Floods of hate, anger, resentment, jealousy cannot obliterate it. It springs back anew with full force.

VERSE 8

We have a little sister,
 and she has no breasts.
What shall we do for our sister,
 on the day when she is spoken for?

The Soul and God answer together:

VERSE 9

If she is a wall,
 we will build upon her a battlement [*buttress*] of
 silver;
but if she is a door,
 we will enclose her with boards of cedar.

Again we have the collective unconscious asking a question of the Bride, who now has consummated her marriage with the Bridegroom. The Soul and the Source are One. The many questions offered to a mystic are not easily answered, for the mystic is in a higher dimension than the questioner; as a result, there is difficulty in answering the questions in simple terms.

The little sister is the immature feminine aspect of man and woman. The further we are from Oneness, the less of this feminine we express. Feminine symbolizes love, intuition, creativity, kindness, pliability. When our feminine is not expressing in a mature way, we do not have the means (breasts) to express these traits. The questions are: ''When our feminine nature wants to start the process of being married to God but cannot express, what shall we do? When we are 'spoken for,' then our feminine is aroused

—but since love, food from the Soul for ourselves and others, seems to have no growth, what can we do?"

God and the Soul are married now. So the answer comes from their Oneness. This is one of the challenges, learning experiences, we may go through after we have given our all to God: how to answer as One and not as two.

The esotericist considers silver as feminine potency and gold as masculine. So if the sister, the immature feminine quality, is a wall, it may be a protection. Or it may be a block to reaching the outside—delay, resistance, or limitation. The wall represents the feminine element.

The feminine element needs to be supported, to be propped up, and we, the Soul and God, help build this of silver or of a highly precious form of the feminine. Thus as we have the feminine in our psyche, and it seems to be falling down, then through love, the high feminine, it will be supported (a buttress built)—it will be helped to stand.

"But if she is a door" is another allusion to the feminine. The door is a feminine symbol. It allows entrance into the privacy of the psyche. While the wall seems to protect, the door allows access to the inner domain. Entrance through the wall is impossible. So if the feminine is a door, it is more readily accessible, and engagement will evolve to the wedding. To open the door is to open the heart, and if the "little sister" is a door, she is much more open to the groom's entering. The groom is also love.

The feminine, the Soul, is here being discussed as immature. The feminine can be a wall that needs more feminine ideas to support it, or it can be a door that is capable of opening and closing. Thus the feminine opens, and the building of the Light body occurs. Then the little sister will reach maturity as the Bride has done.

The Bride speaks:

VERSE 10

> I was a wall,
> and my breasts were like towers;
> then I was in his eyes
> as one who brings [*finds*] peace [*contentment*].

As a wall, the feminine developed the Love chakra, which lies between the breasts, and her love expanded and found peace. God, ever alert to our growth, sees the Soul capable of bringing peace, finding contentment. This is the natural feminine at one with the masculine. It feeds the world with its stately towers of love.

VERSE 11

> Solomon had a vineyard at Baal-hamon;

Baal worship by the Canaanites was considered as sin by the Jews. Baal was the male deity, and Ashtoreth was their principal female deity. Their worship was of nature. Baal symbolizes the worship of materialism—so the Hebrews taught. Baal-Hamon symbolizes a place of the multitude, and the worshippers of Baal/Ashtoreth believe that the source of life and substance is in the outer world. Thus do the millions of humankind now believe. Solomon (God) has a vineyard (vine symbolizes Israel, Israel symbolizes spiritual consciousness). The vineyard is a place of spiritual consciousness in the physical world.

VERSE 11 (cont'd)

> he let out the vineyard to keepers;

We, you, and I, are keepers of the spiritual consciousness, which is God incarnate in each of us.

VERSE 11 (cont'd)

> each one was to bring for its fruit a thousand
> pieces of silver.

There is a price we must pay for spiritual consciousness. We must devote all to God if we are to have the Mystical Marriage or Enlightenment. It is a high price. Here it is symbolized by a thousand pieces of silver. The price is high in human sacrifice, but the price is low in terms of the results.

A thousand brings to our mind the thousand-petaled lotus, or chakra, which is at the crown of the head and in pure light and love as it rays forth. The feminine (silver) is glowing as it is married with the masculine. A thousand rays of light is the result of spiritual consciousness.

VERSE 12

My vineyard, my very own, is for myself;

The Bride speaks. How true, each Soul has its own vineyard, no one else's but only for itself. Each of us is unique. Each of us is a Soul, and no one else can claim our Soul.

VERSE 12 (cont'd)

> you, O Solomon, may have the thousand,
> and the keepers of the fruit two hundred.

You see, after we gain the fruit, we must give it back to our Creator, for it is really His. Our Soul is now one with the Godhead and not selfishly our own. All we have claimed before is no longer ours but belongs to the Universe. The fruit is our spiritual consciousness. The fruit is now God and God gives to all. So our fruit of a thousand is His, belongs to the Universe.

And the keepers of the fruit two hundred. (Verse 12)

The keepers of the fruit are those who have awareness of spiritual consciousness. Awareness is not enough, however, and the Bride sees the amount given to them as much reduced. Two hundred, of course, in numerology reduces to 2, or duality; one thousand reduces to 1, or Oneness, wholeness. At-one-ment is here spoken of as opposed to duality.

The Lover, the Groom, speaks:

VERSE 13

O you who dwell in the gardens,
    my companions are listening for your voice;
    let me hear it.

The garden is, as we have earlier seen, a symbol of the Soul. He always dwells in our Soul; we only need to clear out all the brambles and rubbish that keep us from recognizing this Truth. The Groom, God, is calling out for those in the world who are listening for His voice in their own mind.

Sometimes in this discourse I may have given the impression that God is far off somewhere and that our Soul is wandering around in distant reaches trying to find Him/Her. As we have repeatedly observed, however, God is in the deepest recesses of our Soul. Our task is to remove the distorted consciousness that keeps us from knowing that. The Soul is God. What we are trying to do is get back to that awareness. We are going back to the Garden of Eden where there is no separation. It is Oneness that we all left when we came to duality or earth-living. The task is to overcome that duality and return to Oneness. Then we have served our time on earth and will not need to incarnate in a physical body again. The Soul is allowed to recognize, to be married to its Source. It recognizes the kernel that our thinking has wrapped in husks and shells.

Finally, in "let me hear it," the Lover, or God, is saying, "Let me hear your voice; open up to me, call on me and I will surely answer. Know that I am waiting for your call."

> VERSE 14
>
> Make haste, my beloved,
>   and be like a gazelle
> or a young stag
>   upon the mountains of spices.

"My beloved" is you, is I. It is we of humankind who are being invited to haste to the Kingdom of Heaven—up mountains of spices. We are all invited, we are all capable. We all desire the love and ecstasy, the freedom from pain. In Chapter 21, verses 1–3, of the Book of Revelation we have this description of the final state of our search:

> Then I saw a new heaven and a new earth; for the first heaven and the first earth had passed away and the sea was no more. And I saw the holy city, new Jerusalem, coming down out of heaven from God, prepared as a bride adorned for her husband; and I heard a great voice from the throne saying, "Behold, the dwelling of God is with men. He will dwell with them, and they shall be his people, and God Himself will be with them. . . . "

Then we all shall have reached the Omega Point of Oneness, and we shall all know the love and ecstasy of our Presence.

We are being made aware, day after day, moment by moment, of the rise of the divine feminine in the individual and in society as a whole. What is happening is that the feminine ray of God is becoming more and more active in the earth and in the inhabitants of the earth. This energy touches our Soul, is perhaps a buttress for our Soul, and we are reborn and begin to mature. As we mature spiritually, the balanced symbols of love, the breasts, mature also, and we pour out food for the multitude through love, creativity, compassion, intuition. And the world is healed.

Eventually the whole world will be a part of the Mystic Marriage, and our Omega Point will be reached.

"I am the Alpha and the Omega, the first and the last, the beginning and the end" (Rev. 22:13). God is speaking. He is our beginning as a pure Light body, and He is our end as a pure Light body at One with Him. In the Omega Point of Teilhard de Chardin we are all One. And so it Is, and so it shall Be.

Corinne Heline says (*New Age Bible Interpretation*, vol. 2, p. 162):

> The object of this glorious canticle [*the Song of Songs*] is that it reveals the Shekinah [*feminine wisdom principle*] descended. It shows the history of her in man—the mystery of the Lover and the Beloved throughout the ages of election. . . . And this is the supreme goal of Earth—evolution and the final glorified consummation of the Perfected Way.

And thus it is so! Enlightenment has been reached!

Our Journey may be long and arduous, or it may be joy-filled and easy. Our personal choice and karma make the difference. But whatever the Way may bring, It will end in transformation of the human consciousness into Pure Spiritual consciousness. And that is Ineffable Joy!!

Joy, Joy, Joy
Rises from my heart
And glows in
Eyes and face.

Joy, Joy, Joy
Ethereal and real
Always present at a glance
Or at a second's knowing.

Joy, Joy, Joy
Beyond all words
Expressed only in living
Divinity, as God.

How Joyful is our God
How love-filled, and clear
Of all the negativity
Man has gathered.

Joy, He is Joy
and thus
my Joy
is Supreme.

Epilogue

And so we have come to the end of the Song of Songs. We have learned of the beauty of the experience of Enlightenment. We have learned of the need for meditation, for contemplation. We have learned of the Marriage of the Soul and the Divine Source of all. We have learned of the blockages on the Path. We have seen the Cosmic Being and the Enlightened body of the aspirant. And now the choice is ours. Do we also want this experience as so many mystics have had it, or do we want to stop our searching in this lifetime and wait until an opportunity comes in another life? Are we ready for this Path of self-denial? Do our obligations and attachments allow us to undertake such a divine mission? Do we really want to go all the way? All very personal questions that only each can answer.

This Path, this Climb to Enlightenment, to the Mystic Marriage, will set you apart from most of the people of the world. If you are not willing to take the consequences of your choice, do not begin. "I adjure you, O daughters of Jerusalem . . . that you stir not up nor awaken love until it please" (Song 2:7).

It is a Path of great Joy and Ecstasy. It is a Path of sometimes painful growth, loss of relationships, Dark Night of the Soul, expansion of awareness, aloneness, physical and emotional illness, complete transformation of life both in principles and actions. Your values will change, your morals will change. The purpose for living will change. There will be ups and downs. Glory will shine, then darkness. Your individual choice may go against all the mores of your society. But something calls you when you once start.

The mystic Path choice is the first step. It sounds wonderful, the mystic path, to be guided by the Inner Self that wants only Good for you. And it *is* wonderful and will lead to the greatest happiness, love, and beauty you have ever experienced. But it will not be easy unless you are totally centered in commitment to meditation (listening to the Inner Voice) and are patient.

Overcoming the incrustation of guilt, greed, resentment, anger, hate, sexual lust, sexual cravings, need for close human companionship and others will be part of the glorious adventure, for it is an adventure like no other on earth.

According to those who have been declared Enlightened by the Church and modern judges, it is All-Knowing; overcoming challenges; letting go of prayers of petition; reaching the Omega Point. A wonderful book, *Silent Fire,* * gives excerpts from the writings and the lives of many of these mystical teachers. I should like to quote a few.

St. John of the Cross has this to say about the final step:

> The tenth and last step of this secret ladder of love causes the soul to become wholly assimilated to God, by reason of the clear and immediate vision of God which it now possesses. Of these St. Matthew says, "Blessed are the pure in

Silent Fire: An Invitation to Western Mysticism. Walter Holden Capps and Wendy H. Wright, eds. (New York: Harper & Row, 1978). Copyright © 1978 by Walter Holden Capps and Wendy H. Wright. The quotations that follow are from pp. 195, 49, and 243 respectively. Reprinted by permission of Harper & Row, Publishers, Inc.

heart, for they shall see God." And, as we say, this vision is the cause of the perfect likeness of the soul to God. There is naught that is hidden from the soul, by reason of its complete assimilation.

Bernard of Clairvaux says this, which is helpful as we face our challenges:

> It was not by His motions that He was recognized by me, nor could I tell by any of my senses that He had penetrated to the depths of my being. It was only by the movement of my heart that I was able to recognize His presence, and to know the might of His power by the sudden departure of vices and the strong restraint put upon all carnal affections. [*St. Bernard has written on the mystical interpretation of the Song of Songs.*]

Thomas Merton, a latter-day Enlightened one, says:

> This inner awareness, this experience of love as an immediate and dynamic presence, tends to alter our perspective. We see the prayer of petition a little differently. Celebration and praise, loving attention to the presence of God, become more important than "asking for" things and "getting" things.

And Teresa of Avila, a favorite of mine, writes in the *Interior Castle* (soul):

> Let us now come to treat of the Divine and Spiritual Marriage, although this great favor cannot be fulfilled perfectly in us during our lifetime, for if we were to withdraw ourselves from God this great blessing would be lost. When granting this favor for the first time, His Majesty is pleased to reveal Himself to the soul through an imaginary vision of His most sacred Humanity, so that it may clearly understand what is taking place and not be ignorant of the fact that it is receiving so sovereign a gift.

She also says:

> And: Perhaps when St. Paul says: "He who is joined to God
> becomes one spirit with Him," he is referring to this sover-
> eign Marriage, which presupposes the entrance of His
> Majesty into the soul by union. And he also says: "For me
> to live is Christ, to die is gain." This, I think, the soul may
> say here, for it is here that the little butterfly to which we
> have referred dies, and with the greatest joy, because Christ
> is now its life.

And one last quote from *Interior Castle*:*

> These effects God bestows, together with all those other
> good effects already described in the above-mentioned
> degrees of prayer, when the soul approaches Him, and He
> also gives the soul that kiss for which the Bride besought
> Him, for I understand it to be in this Mansion that that pe-
> tition is fulfilled. Here to this wounded heart are given
> waters in abundance. Here the soul delights in the taberna-
> cle of God.

We must not leave out Teilhard de Chardin, who writes
in his *The Phenomenon of Man*, concerning the "higher
pole of evolution":

> What should this higher pole of evolution be, in order to
> fulfil its role? . . . It is by definition in Omega that—in its
> flower and in its integrity—the hoard of consciousness
> liberated little by little on earth by noogenesiss itself
> together and concentrates. [Noogenesis *means birth and de-*
> *velopment of mind as a transforming agency.*] . . . The
> very center of our consciousness, deeper than all its radii;

---

*All quotations are from St. Teresa of Avila, *Interior Castle*. E. Allison
Peers, ed. and trans. (Garden City, N.Y.: Image Books, 1961), pp. 185,
186, 224.

that is the essence which Omega, if it is to be truly Omega, must reclaim. . . . For we are the very flame of that torch.*

We have all the evidence that we need from writers and speakers of the need for the ascendancy of man to Oneness with his Creator. The Song of Songs has corroborated that statement. And so let us search for the Path that best fits us for this high Estate—Oneness with our own Divinity.

"He who conquers and who keeps my works until the end, I will give him power over the nations . . . and I will give him the morning star" (Rev. 2:26, 28. *Morning star* is Enlightenment. Jesus is speaking here).

---

*Pierre Teilhard de Chardin, *The Phenomenon of Man* (New York: Harper & Row, 1965), pp. 260, 261. Copyright © 1955 by Editions du Seuil. Copyright © 1959 in the English translation by William Collins Sons & Company and Harper & Row, Publishers, Inc. Reprinted by permission of Harper & Row, Publishers, Inc.

Enlightenment

What is it?

This question has never been fully answered by man or woman, for it cannot be answered in so many words, metaphors, or similes. Like our physical being, it is beyond description. The human body is still a mystery.

We believe that Enlightenment is real—or at least that it is possible for a man or a woman to experience it. But what it is lies beyond our intellect to assimilate.

Enlightenment. Such an esoteric term. How difficult to explain it! It is used rather freely, as in "This should be enlightening to you" or "I have been enlightened by your remarks." But what is Enlightenment?

I have discussed Enlightenment throughout this book. However, for your "enlightenment" I should like to add a few remarks.

Many have aspired to the experience and have withdrawn from society to study, to meditate, to become more deeply aware of the spiritual side of their consciousness. Even today, in this time of "new" thought and inquiry, many are aspiring to this condition. Why? Why is it so important?

There are those who teach, from the personal experience, such as Gopi Krishna, that all of humankind has the potential to arrive at this high state, and thus that humanity will return to the Perfection of Being as taught by all great religious Masters. Pierre Teilhard de Chardin is another great teacher who believed that humanity would finally reach the Omega Point of Oneness with Divinity.

So what is it to be Englightened—fully, completely filled with Light—?

Unconsciously, we all know in the deepest recesses of our Soul that human life is somewhere between the animal and what we call the Divine. Somehow we each know that there is an existence at a higher, though deeper, level that we are experiencing on this earth. It seems to be innate and inexplicable. And no matter how our great teachers have tried to explain it to us, we reduce it to our own level of consciousness.

Jesus called it "The Kingdom of Heaven." Catholic saints called it the Unitive Life or the Mystical Marriage. Some Christians call it Cosmic Consciousness. The Zen Buddhist calls it Satori. Some Buddhists call it Bodhi. The Sufis call it Fana. The Muslims call it Heaven. The Taoist calls it "The Ultimate Tao," or *wu*. The Hindus and Tibetans call it Samadhi or Moksha. It is perfection and freedom from all the ills we experience on earth.

Many humans have used drugs as well as various incantations by other human beings designated as gurus, masters, teachers, shamans, medicine men, etc., to evoke this state. The flash of the experience is deeply felt and experienced, but it is usually short-lived. It is agreed by most teachers that it is a long, arduous journey to reach this perfect state of awareness of our so-called Divinity. It may take many lifetimes or occur in the present one. But it is not a magic flash that has not been earned.

One of the best ways to answer the question "What is

Enlightenment?'' is to read the accounts of the experience that others have left for us. Some of them are:

Mysticism, by Evelyn Underhill
Cosmic Consciousness, by Maurice Bucke
The Interior Castle, by St. Teresa of Avila
Dark Night of the Soul, by St. John of the Cross
Life and Teaching of the Masters of the Far East, by Baird
   T. Spalding
The Works of Bernard of Clairvaux on the Song of Songs. *

Some of the most enlightened never wrote anything or spoke with anyone else about the experience. Some of those claiming Enlightenment today do not measure up to the descriptions given by saints and advanced Souls. We can be fooled by claiming for ourselves a high level of awareness without being truly enlightened. At the same time we should accept our Divinity.

One seeking Enlightenment is called a mystic. However, there are those who do not recognize that they are mystics and have an experience of Enlightenment. This experience may bring them to the realization of their true Path. A mystic is one who has accepted his/her divine duty to live for God only.

The mystic is on his/her way but may not be Enlightened. The humble man or woman fulfilling responsibilities on earth may be far more advanced than the leader of a particular religious organization. We cannot always measure the height or depth of consciousness by the outer trappings.

*All of these are listed in the Bibliography.

Enlightenment comes as a result of the Grace of God and the potential of the Seeker who has given over his personal will to the Will of that Divinity which is within her/his Soul. It is a reward. It is an achievement. It comes by renunciation, by devotion, by Centeredness on the Christ, on the All. It is freely given but earned. It is gained by the overcoming of attachment to things and people of the world and a "throwing in" with that Inexplicable Power which we know but do not understand.

And so what is Enlightenment?

It is knowing that I know because I am That which Is. It is certainty without doubt. It is beyond scientific and physical proof. It is not replicable by any action on my part. It is a gift. It is reaching beyond what most call conscious knowing into a superconscious realm. It is mysterious and yet fully understood. It is a paradox. But it is more. It is more Real than any other experience we can have. And it changes the seeker completely. But the experience may not be at the highest level that can be achieved. It may happen again and again at higher levels. The end lies in Infinity. It is beyond our human understanding. It is Oneness with all that Is.

Enlightenments may vary from religion to religion, from culture to culture, for the experience comes from different standards of behavior, beliefs, and mores. But the experience has many commonalities, for in the ultimate all human beings are the same, are all One.

Are you Enlightened? Well, I think you would know if you were. However, you might measure yourself against the life and the teachings of Jesus Christ as a model. Some say if you are completely free of avarice, greed, and anger and are centered in love, forgiveness, and charity to all, you have reached at least one stage of Enlightenment. In any case, each will know deep within his Soul if he is ready for the step of being One with God. But no one can teach you how or when it will happen. It is an inside job.

Without doubt you will know the answer to the questions, Who am I? Why am I here? Where am I going? What is life all about? You will have arrived at the answers and be living in the answers. For all questions will lie dormant in the Presence of All That Is.

Enlightenment is total freedom. It is freedom from fear, anxiety, sorrow, and attachment. It is gaiety and laughter. It is Pure Joy. It is becoming as a little child. It is complete freedom from fear of death. It brings the ability to move from one state of consciousness to another. It may be the changing of the molecular structure of your physical body, so that Pure Light shines through. And seeking it is a Path that should be entered upon only for the purpose of serving God and man. For it is an unselfish seeking and it often happens without foreknowledge or previous experience. And last but not least, it is a Knowing of the Universality of all that is. Then one can say, "I am God" with absolute conviction, for thus it is. "I am God" and "God is I." All one Truth.

What more can be said? Much more, but I will end by quoting Jalalu'd Din (Rumi):

With Thy Sweet Soul, this soul of mine
  Hath mixed as Water doth with Wine.
Who can the Wine and Water part,
  Or me and Thee when we combine?
Thou art become my greater self;
  Small bounds no more can me confine.
Thou hast my being taken on,
  And shall I not take on Thine?

Me Thou for ever hast affirmed,
  That I may ever know Thee mine.
Thy love has pierced me through and through,
  Its thrill with bone and Nerve entwine.
I rest a Flute laid on Thy lips;
  A lute, I on Thy breast recline.
Breathe deep in me that I may sigh;
  Yet strike my strings, and tears shall shine.*

*Jalalu'd Din, "The Festival of Spring," quoted in Evelyn Underhill, *Mysticism* (Cleveland: World Publishing Co., 1967), p. 426.

Glossary

ADEPT—One who has arrived; thoroughly proficient; an expert; Enlightened; knows God face to face.

ANDROGYNY—A state of perfect balance between the masculine and the feminine in our psyche. Innate sense of cosmic unity; Oneness; Wholeness.

ANIMA—The feminine element within a man's psyche. (See Jung's psychology.)

ANIMUS—The inner contrasexual, masculine element within a woman's psyche. (See Jung's psychology.)

CHAKRAS—Centers or whirls of energy in central locations in the ethereal (energy or auric) body or spirit body. They are connected to the physical body at the location of the endocrine glands.

CHRIST—The spark of Divinity within each consciousness. The Inner Voice, the Counselor; Mighty God; Everlasting Father; Prince of Peace (Isaiah 9:6). Jesus called it the Father.

COLLECTIVE UNCONSCIOUS—The totality of beliefs, thoughts, memories, feelings, and experiences of the human race.

CONSCIOUSNESS—Conscious awareness of God, of the Spirit.

ENLIGHTENMENT—"A condition in which all connections with the world are absorbed into the Inner World" (Carl Jung). Mystical Marriage; result of soul and Spirit reaching Oneness.

GENERATION—To procreate, to beget, to reproduce.

INITIATE—New-born after conversion; a voluntary laying down of the personal life for the spiritual life; one who is a servant of servants, a teacher of teachers.

KUNDALINI—An Eastern word for Divine Energy. The serpent fire of regeneration lying at the base of the spine. The spine is the path up which it travels to regenerate the physical body, to change the physical to Light, or spiritual essence.

MYSTIC—One who has accepted his/her divine duty to live for God only.

NEOPHYTE, ASPIRANT—The beginner on the Path.

"OLD" SOUL—A mature soul, a product of evolution, rich in wisdom learned in former lives or through "special" instruction.

RACE CONSCIOUSNESS—The beliefs, actions, mores of that society in which we live that affect our choices.

REGENERATION—Transforming the physical into the spiritual.

SOUL—Inner Christ; the spark of the Divine indwelling human consciousness.

Bibliography

Alder, Vera Stanley. *The Finding of the Third Eye*. York Beach, Maine: Samuel Weiser, 1938.

Bernard of Clairvaux. *The Works of Bernard of Clairvaux on the Song of Songs*. Kalamazoo, Mich.: Cistercian Publications, 1976.

Bucke, Richard Maurice, M.D. *Cosmic Consciousness*. New York: E.P. Dutton, 1969.

Capps, Walter Holden, and Wendy M. Wright. *Silent Fire*. San Francisco: Harper & Row, 1978.

Elder, Dorothy. *Revelation: For a New Age* (The Book of Revelation). Marina del Rey, Calif.: DeVorss & Company, 1981.

Fillmore, Charles. *Jesus Christ Heals*. Unity Village, Mo.: Unity School of Christianity, 1939.

Fillmore, Charles. *Metaphysical Bible Dictionary*. Unity Village, Mo.: Unity School of Christianity, 1931.

Ghanananda (Swami), and Sir John Stewart Wallace. *Women Saints of East and West*. Hollywood: Vedanta Press, 1979.

Hall, Manly P. *Old Testament Wisdom*. Los Angeles: Philosophical Research Society, 1957.

Heline, Corinne. *New Age Bible Interpretation* (7 vols.). Los Angeles: New Age Press, 1935–1954.

Hopkins, Emma Curtis. *High Mysticism*. Marina del Rey, Calif.: DeVorss & Company, 1974.

John of the Cross. *Dark Night of the Soul*. Garden City, N.Y.: Image Books, 1959.

Jung, Carl. *Psychology and Religion: West and East* (Bollingen Series XX). Princeton, N.J.: Princeton University Press, 1969.

Krishna, Gopi. *Kundalini: The Evolutionary Energy*. Boston: Shambhala Publications, 1970.

Pope, Marvin H. *Song of Songs Based on Anchor Bible*. Garden City, N.Y.: Doubleday, 1977.

Progoff, Ira. *The Cloud of Unknowing*. New York: Dell Publishing Co., 1983.

Spalding, Baird T. *Life and Teaching of the Masters of the Far East*. Marina del Rey, Calif.: DeVorss & Company, 1964.

Stone, Merlin. *When God Was a Woman*. San Diego: Harcourt Brace Jovanovich, 1976.

Teilhard de Chardin, Pierre. *The Phenomenon of Man*. New York: Harper & Row, 1965.

Teresa of Avila. *Interior Castle*. Garden City, N.Y.: Doubleday, 1961.

Underhill, Evelyn. *Mysticism*. Cleveland: World Publishing Company, 1967.

White, John (ed.). *What Is Enlightenment? Exploring the Call of the Spiritual Path*. Los Angeles: Jeremy P. Tarcher, 1984.